HIS HEART, MY HEART

Devotional Transformation

HIS HEART, MY HEART
DEVOTIONAL TRANSFORMATION

MICHAEL PARROTT

To the 1978-1981 Faculty
at Western Seminary who
increased my love for God, His Word, and
taught me how to handle God's Word.

CONTENTS

Contents

PREFACE

REAL LIFE STORIES

It was thirteen years ago that I first put the book you hold in your hands in print. It first appeared at the end of my class notes for my Discipleship class and then became a separate book a few years later. Since that time over 500 men and women have field tested it and several changes have been made based upon their comments. As I evaluated the effectiveness of this tool with my students I discovered that those who did at least 70% of the devotionals on a daily basis saw significant Christ-like transformation in his or her convictions, character, and conduct. Also, I discovered that those who met in small groups each week to discuss the previous seven days they had completed in this devotional on devotions increased their grace and knowledge of Jesus Christ. Finally, those who also met one-on-one to discuss their progress were more faithful to complete this due to being accountable to someone.

Because the devotional life develops as one moves through the stages of discipleship, I thought you might be interested in reading some of the stories of these adults after completing this training tool. Besides, it might help you identify where you are in the stages of discipleship and what you can hope to discover from working your way through this book.

NEW DISCIPLES

"Before doing this devotional life project, my perception of the concept of devotions and the devotional life was very basic. There was never a real emphasis on devotions in my house growing up. I did grow up in a Christian home, going to church every week, very involved in youth group, and even my parents were very involved in my youth group as well. I knew that my parents did devotions every morning at six. However, they never really encouraged me to do devotions or read my Bible or anything like that. None of that was really emphasized in my youth group either, or even my church. After doing this devotional, all the lessons that I've learned about devotions have been reinforced. The importance of knowing God's heart and aligning mine with His is a huge one. I can't just read about Him, I really must *want* Him. I must *seek* Him. I must *long* for Him. That's the main difference between my view of devotions before and after this project."   — Adam

"Through this devotional I have recognized my need for time with Him and that it needs to be consistent to promote the most potential growth. In the beginning, it was a challenge to do it every day. But, as I continued to go through this devotional it became easier to spend time daily with God. This devotional allowed me to regain my desire for God's Word and for intentional time with Him. I know one aspect that will have to continue is to not only read the passage, but to have an application to follow. I found that my time with God is precious and days I don't spend with Him, are days where my attitude or actions are not in line with His. From this devotional, I have gained a consistent time with Him and a new perspective on the devotional life, which I realize is still a work in progress and will take time to perfect. Overall, I felt this devotional was what I needed as a guide to refocus and realign my heart to God's. Also, this devotional has changed the way I go about studying God's Word and prayer. My quiet time has moved from something I knew I should do to something that I need and want to do. I have a desire and a longing for God's Word and to grow in my personal walk with Him that has been missing. Through this devotional I have seen that to be like Christ and to have our hearts aligned with His, we have to have consistent time with Him."   —Maddie

"Before going through the His Heart, My Heart devotional, I had a very vague understanding of what the devotional life was all about. In fact, I had never even heard it referred to as the devotional life, nor did I realize that prayer was the primary key to its success. I didn't have a very disciplined routine of spending time with God; I usually read a passage from the Bible, prayed for current needs and issues in my life and the lives around me, and maybe jotted a verse or two down in a journal that stuck out to me that day. As I went through the devotional, I began to see from the life of Jesus that prayer is what constitutes the devotional life. It's how Jesus connected with the Father to receive His will and carry it out each day during His earthly ministry. I also began to see the depth of meaning in the words of the Lord's Prayer in Matthew 6:9-13. We had prayed that prayer so often in my church growing up that I didn't truly meditate on the words or pray it genuinely from my heart. Asking the Father for our daily bread comes out of trust in His name and attributes. Comparing our hearts to the standard of His Kingdom convicts us to confess our sins, receive His forgiveness, and forgive others. Desiring God's will to be done here on earth, both in our hearts and environments, draws us to depend on the Holy Spirit to accomplish God's will and resist

11

temptation from the evil one."   —Kelton

GROWING DISCIPLES

"Before I started to do the devotional, I found myself in a stagnant place of worship. I was doing quiet time every day, I was pushing others to grow in different ways while watching some grow closer to the Lord. At that time, I didn't really see myself growing any closer to Him. I wasn't sure what I was doing wrong and why I wasn't seeing growth in my own personal life. When I started doing this book, many of the topics that were coming up in the beginning seemed very basic and things that I thought I was already well-versed in. As I started working my way through them more and more, I started to realize that I may know many different facts about certain subjects, but how much was I actually prayerfully considering the different topics? The book was really huge in motivating me to realize that the time I spend with God needs to be adjusted so that I am acting in a way that is realizing all the different aspects of who God actually is. Taking time to see God as king and as Father makes things so much more intimate. Time with God is so much better now."   —Alex

"This Devotional made it clear that prayer should be done throughout the devotional time. Another part of prayer that was evidenced in this devotional was intercessory prayer. I hadn't really prayed intercessory prayers during my personal devotional time but this devotional encouraged me to do it. This has led to a really cool community focus even when I'm on my own and a way to get the focus off myself and on to my brothers and sisters in Christ. It was a really neat experience to slow down and focus on parts of verses each day. For my regular devotions, I usually focus on 3-10 verses and focus in on them. This brought my focus form a magnified glass to a microscope and it was a joy to see how interwoven scripture is even at the smallest level. This book also changed some of the way I go about studying a passage. It is important to study individual passages and individual books of the bible but if we don't see all the smaller texts joining into one big TEXT then we have missed a valuable point."   — Mitchell

"While going through this devotional I struggled with being honest with God. There were some sections in the book which asked me to think on certain issues and I would often be tempted to rationalize those sins away in my head. I would tell myself those issues were not that bad and I should just forget about them. This is the wrong approach to have however. I should not be trying to avoid confessing my sins to the Lord. When I started to be more honest with myself and with God, the devotionals started to greatly resonate in my heart. Beginning this devotional and keeping up with it was hard for the first week or so. When I started to be more honest with myself I found it easier to do. I soon found myself doing the devotional daily and even on the weekends."   —Erica

"Adoring God was being reinforced as I went through this devotional. I know that I need to tell God who He is to set my mind on Him and humble myself to get ready to spend time with Him. Some new things that I discovered in this is the real emphasis I need to start placing on praying for others. I have always been quick to want to pray for others when they have brought requests to me but I have not been one to keep them on a prayer list and pray for them each day. I have always had the idea of doing this but I never put it into practice like I did these past forty days. I think it has been good for me. I love my friends and family and even people I don't know and it's been great to be able to take these forty days and really pray for them and be diligent and disciplined in that. I think some adjustments God is asking me to make in my devotional life is honestly the consistency in my quiet time with Him. I am quick to jump over passages or even skip a few days because I don't feel as if I am really benefitting from it. This past year I have been doing a lot better at spending intentional daily time with God but I have not been good at sticking with a book of the bible and reading through it. I am quick to change because I don't feel like it is speaking to me now. I have learned that God is going to speak to us through His Word and that it is important to stay diligent and learn what He says even if I don't have any immediate applications. It is important for building my knowledge of Him so that I am more knowledgeable about God and His purposes but also so I can help others because I have read and know where to take them in the Bible when they have questions or need some encouragement." —Lora

MATURE DISCIPLES

"During the first few days, the things I learned were more reinforcements of principles rather than brand new concepts. Such as the idea that prayer is the high priority or the importance of a quiet time in general. However. there were several adjustments that I had to make throughout the process, such as adjusting my proper focus towards God and remembering that my quiet time is before the throne—that my prayer is before the God of heaven and that He cares to listen to me at all, which is a beautiful truth that really made me realign my thoughts. While this was something I sort of already new through my years of going to church, it was the first time it really sunk into me. One of the ideas that was brand new to me, was the idea of praying out loud. The first few days go into the importance of finding a quiet, secluded place of prayer and then discussed that this is so one can freely talk out loud in conversation with God, since most of the prayers in the Old Testament were spoken out loud. This was something that I had never really considered before, praying aloud, since I had always prayed privately inside my mind. Also, the idea of finding a big idea for every Bible reading was also a new idea for me. I had never been taught to bring that level of intentionality into a daily quiet time, and I enjoyed taking that opportunity. I learned a lot through this devotional, learning new concepts, adjusting old assumptions in my prayer time, and reinforcing truths that I had been slacking on during my quiet time. I was really glad I had the opportunity to go through this devotional and I feel like my devotional times are more structured. This experience taught me much about how to have a consistent, structured bible study." —Sharon

MULTIPLYING DISCIPLES

"Before starting 'His Heart, My Heart' I never realized how in-depth the devotional life was. I am a person of habit. It takes me a long time to form them and even longer to change or add to them. My devotional time took me awhile to build but it is even harder for me to change it. I was nervous about starting this because I thought that would have to change the way I did everything and nothing would stick. I also did not realize how significant little changes in actions from what I was already doing would change my heart so much. After going through this devotional, I realized that many of things I already knew or I was already doing some of them. I did not need to alter my whole devotional time. I just needed to change small things. However, these small things really helped fine tune things I was already

15

doing in my time with the Lord. This change also helped me look at my devotional time with a fresh perspective. It made it fun and exciting rather than being the same thing. I love opening up this book each day. I knew almost all of these things but I was not practicing them all. Being heavenly-mind was something that I knew was important but I was not living heavenly minded each day. I am still not every second of every day being heavenly minded but now I am more aware of that and have been more heavenly minded each day. This has been a huge shift in thinking, which has brought me closer to the Lord in my daily life. The devotional development section of this book was so helpful for me. I struggled to take knowledge and apply it well and this part helped me to grow in doing this. This really helped kick start my devotional time and the way that I apply it. It really helped be grow and as well as track it. Even by writing this all down I see what God is teaching and showing me."

—Serafina

Each of these adults have seen their devotional life transformed and as a result, their lives are daily being transformed into His image for His purposes. The practice of a Biblical Devotional life is a daily revival of God's life in a believer. Dr. Walter Kaiser says, "Without prayer, revivals do not even begin."[1] You should think of the devotional life of prayer as the first place God starts to renew and refresh His work in us personally before He awakens the world. As I sat under the teaching of J. Edwin Orr back in 1974 and heard him speak of revivals and awakenings throughout history I was captivated by how God through His Holy Spirit changes individuals, churches, communities and the world as believers align

---

[1] Walter C. Kaiser, Jr., *Revive Us Again* (Scotland, Christian Focus, 2001), 30.

their hearts and lives with God's heart. Orr says,

> An Evangelical Awakening is a movement of the
> Holy Spirit bringing about a revival of New
> Testament Christianity in the Church of Christ
> and in its related community.[2]

It is with this in mind that I offer this tool to you. May
God bring life afresh to believers worldwide and may He
begin it with you today. Are you ready for a devotional
transformation?

---

[2] J. Edwin Orr, *The Fervent Prayer* (Chicago, IL: Moody
Press, 1974), vii.

WALKING IN STEP WITH THE HOLY SPIRIT

"Come, let us worship and bow down, let us kneel before the Lord our Maker. For He is our God, and we are the people of His pasture and the sheep of His hand. Today, if you would hear His voice, do not harden your hearts, as at Meribah, as in the day of Massah in the wilderness, when your fathers tested Me, they tried Me, though they had seen My work."
—*Psalm 95:6-9*

"Because you are sons, God has sent forth the Spirit of His Son into our hearts, crying, 'Abba! Father!' Therefore, you are no longer a slave, but a son; and if a son, then an heir through God."
—*Galatians 4:6-7*

"Did you hear it this morning?" one of my students eagerly asked after stopping me in the corridor of our guest house in Kenya. Her abrupt question caused my mind to jump from one thought to another thought as I tried to imagine what she had heard. When nothing came to mind, I asked, "Hear what?" "That man talking on a loudspeaker, it sounded like it was right outside my room." This was our team's first morning in Africa and the guest house we were staying in was right next to a Mosque. What she heard was the 5 am call to prayer.

Religions rely upon external motivation to promote

obedience among its adherents but Christianity is different. It is not based on duty but delight in an eternal relationship with God. It is a relationship where God lives within every believer and motivates the believer internally to act.

HEAR HIM

When Paul wrote to the Galatians after they had just come to faith in Christ during his first missionary journey he identifies one of the first signs of spiritual life as this internal prompting in Galatians 4:6, "Because you are sons, God has sent forth the Spirit of His Son into our hearts, crying, 'Abba! Father!'" God takes up residence within every believer in Christ and draws that disciple into communication with God as his or her Father.

God is at work in you! If you have accepted Jesus' sacrifice on the cross as payment for your sins, then you have resurrection life dwelling in you – the same power that raised Jesus from the grave to show that His sacrifice satisfied God's anger towards sin. Because of His indwelling presence in you, He draws you into communication with God. He initiates the devotional life. He moves you to desire to speak with God as your Father. If you are in His family, you have access to the Father's presence and will desire to speak with Him. This is supernaturally prompted and sustained by the Holy Spirit living in you.

So, the only question is, "Did you hear Him today?" Do you understand what I am asking you? Just to be clear here, if you are a believer, a follower of Jesus Christ, a disciple, you will sense Him drawing you into communication with God as your Father. This is a supernatural vital sign of having spiritual life, a new nature, the indwelling presence of God in you, of you truly being a child of God. So, let me ask you again, "Have you heard Him today?" "Have you sensed a desire to talk with Him?" And, "When you have sensed Him giving you the thought of spending time with the Father what have you done with it?"

HEED HIM

Paul reminds the Philippian believers in Philippians 2:12-16 about the need to continue to respond to God:

> So, then, my beloved, just as you have always obeyed, not as in my presence only, but now much more in my absence, work out your salvation with fear and trembling; for it is God who is at work in you, both to will and to work for His good pleasure. Do all things without grumbling of disputing; so that you will prove yourselves to be blameless and innocent, children of God above reproach in the midst of a crooked and perverse generation, among whom you appear as lights in the world, holding fast the word of life, so that in the day of Christ I will have reason to glory because I did not run nor toil in vain.

As you work out (i.e. live out) the salvation that God has already worked within you, you will begin living your life for Him and be the light in the world for Him that you were designed to be. Perhaps you are doing well with this now. But who is helping you stay on mission?

Paul notes that the Philippian believers were to do this whether Paul was physically present with them or not. It is easy sometimes to appear to walk with God when your mentor or a more mature believer is around, but sometimes we lack the motivation to continue when they are gone. However, Paul combats this problem by noting that they are to act in obedience with fear and trembling in Philippians 2:12 and then explains why in the very next verse (v.13).

Introduction

Obviously being moved by the adrenaline that fear produces and feeling it to the core of our being so that we experience a physical trembling shows that "fear" can be a powerful motivator. But this "fear" isn't to immobilize us or cause us to flee. It is to actually draw us towards God. So why should we have this response? What should grab our attention and move us?

Notice that the text says that since God Himself is living in us and producing the desire to do His will and the ability to do it there should be a holy reverence towards His work in our lives. We cannot escape His presence. He is living in us. Therefore, the reason for the response of "fear" and "trembling" is the recognition of who we are responding to – God. It is His promptings that we are experiencing! So, how should we treat Him?

Paul knows the flesh is weak and that although God is at work in us producing the desire and the ability we are still the ones who make a choice. Knowing this, it seems that Paul anticipates how we will tend to respond at first. According to Philippians 2:14 how might we respond? The text says, "Do all things without grumbling or disputing." Seriously? Paul knows that even though it is God working in us, we can fail to respond appropriately. Paul indicates that we can – under our breath – refuse to cooperate with what God is trying to do by grumbling or we can outwardly rebel against Him with open disputing.

So, when God prompts the thought in you to open your Bible and spend some time in communication with your heavenly Father, what is your response? Do you under your breath grumble about it? Do you try to resist it and even come up with all kinds of reasons not to listen? Or do you openly dispute what He is doing even blaming others for suggesting or requiring you to meet with God?

The writer to the Hebrews, in Hebrews 4:7b says, "Today if you hear His voice, do not harden your hearts." If we fail to say "yes" to God's promptings, His voice crying "Abba! Father!" – which I should note is a loud cry like a baby's cry and not a quiet voice – and we resist or rebel against Him instead of responding in delight, think about who it is that you are really resisting and rebelling against!

Responding to God

Paul again identifies who is working in a believer's life in Ephesians 4:30, saying, "Do not grieve the Holy Spirit of God, by whom you were sealed for the day of redemption." We can grieve the work of God in our lives by saying "no" to Him. He also notes that we can put a stop to His work in our lives according to I Thessalonians 5:19 which says, "Do not quench the Spirit." This has the idea of putting out a fire. As God is drawing you to Himself, you can actually put out the promptings, the cry, by deliberately choosing not to respond!

When any of these things happen, we need to confess our sin to God. Think about what John says in I John 1:9, "If we confess our sin, He is faithful and righteous to forgive us our sins and to cleanse us from all unrighteousness." Once we admit our error and seek to turn from it back to Him and what He is doing then we will again have fellowship with our Father and the blood of Jesus will keep in check our sinful disposition from exerting itself in more sinful acts – this is the idea of the term "cleansing" us from all sin in I John 1:7.

Daily Walking With God

So, since God is in us, moving us to want what He wants and giving us the ability to do what He asks (Philippians 2:13), how can we consistently, daily, get on board with what God is working to do in and through us? How can we continually and willingly align our hearts with His heart? How can we know His will for us and do it?

Paul discusses this in Ephesians 5:15-21, where he

says,

> Therefore, be careful how you walk, not as unwise
> men but as wise, making the most of your time,
> because the days are evil. So then do not be
> foolish, but understand what the will of the Lord
> is. And do not get drunk with wine, for that is
> dissipation, but be filled with the Spirit, speaking
> to one another in psalms and hymns and spiritual
> songs, singing and making melody with your
> heart to the Lord; always giving thanks for all
> things in the name of our Lord Jesus Christ to
> God, even the Father; and being subject to one
> another in the fear of Christ.

This passage needs some unpacking or explanation.
First, note the contrast between being "wise" and
"unwise". What is it that the "wise" do that the "unwise"
person doesn't do? One thing a wise believer does is that
they are "careful" how they walk. Another thing he or she
does is make the most of their time.

A few comments are in order here about this phrase.
The word used for "time" here refers to opportunities
(Kairos) not to the passing of time (Chronos). Paul is
referring here to specific opportunities to do something.
Teddy Roosevelt once said, "Opportunity is like a horse,
it gallops up, pauses for a moment, gives you a chance to
get on and then gallops off." That actually captures the
idea of "kairos" or time here in this passage.
Opportunities are those uniquely divine moments of life
that come up unexpectedly and then can just as quickly
vanish. What is to be done with them?

The idea here of "making the most of your time or
opportunities" can be misleading as the text isn't saying
cramp more things into your already full schedule. The
wording here is really "redeem the time" or "redeem the
opportunities". Or in other words, "purchase out of

bondage to the evil one the opportunities by doing God's will in their place".

The idea based on the context of the entire book of Ephesians in that this world is in bondage to the evil one as explained in Ephesians 2:1-3 and sinful attitudes and actions prevail in the world because of this. Here in Ephesians 5:15-16 Paul is saying that with every opportunity that comes our way the believer's role is to purchase back what is in bondage to the evil one for God. How do we do this?

The first step is to "understand what the will of the Lord is" in a given situation as noted in verse 17. What is God's will? What does He want in the given situation? Where do we find that? We find it in His word – the Hebrew, Aramaic, and Greek Scriptures – the sixty-six books of the Bible. When we properly handle God's Word we discover His truths, His will, and the life context in which they are to be applied.

This is an important process: accurately handling God's Word. It is easy today to take truths out of their context and even once understood to misapply them outside of the life context in which the author intended for them to be used. This takes some additional training and so I have included in Appendix Three some basic training on this. For more detailed training please refer to my book, *Transformed by Truth* and visit my website: www.hisheartmyheart.org for helpful training and tools to see how to sustain biblical transformation through using only God's Word.

The second step is to allow the Holy Spirit – who is producing the desire to want His will and giving you the ability to do it according to Philippians 2:13 – to have His way in your life. Submit to Him. Ask Him to control you and empower you. Ask Him to give you the desire and ability to do what He wants. That is what Paul has in mind here with this command in Ephesians 5:18, "Be

Introduction
filled with the Spirit".

Realize that you are asking God to do what He already wants to do. That is biblical faith. Trusting God to do His word in you. It is trusting Him at His word. Biblical faith is not wishful thinking, a leap, or without reliable evidence. It is acting in alignment with the evidence, it is trusting in a reliable object of faith, and in this case, it is God and His Word.

Maybe you have wondered how you will know if you are filled with the Spirit. According to this passage there are two practical evidences that you are by faith trusting that God has empowered you. First, there is a specific evidence – you can now supernaturally do what His word says (cf. v17). If you resisted or rebelled against God and His word and you confessed your sin in doing this, you should now be able in God's Spirit to turn around and immediately do His Word (His will) in His power in the current opportunity before you. So, if you resisted or rebelled against His crying "Abba! Father!" and drawing you into communication with Him you should now (immediately) be able to spend time with God in response to His work in your life.

In the same way, with any scripture you read and understand, you will now in His supernatural power be able to desire it and do it and thus create a God moment in the midst of a moment that is in bondage to the evil one and thus rescue it for God's purposes and glory. But remember, there is a real battle, a spiritual battle, that you are facing in every opportunity. You may want to read Ephesians 6:10-18 and think more about this and how to be more effective for God and His purposes during this battle for each opportunity.

Second, there is a general evidence of you depending upon the Holy Spirit. You will find yourself in the fellowship of others speaking with joy and song to one another, giving thanks for all things, and subjecting yourself to one another (Ephesians 5:19-21). This is the general evidence of being filled with the Holy Spirit as others experience your blessed presence because your life is aligned with God's and you have done and are doing in His strength His will in this world that is in bondage to the evil one.

NEXT STEPS

Where do we go from here? First, if you practice the truths noted above in God's power you will be experiencing in microcosm the very essence of the devotional life. You will walk with God, overcome the evil one, and bring God's will to bear upon the opportunities He gives you to address in this world all to His glory.

Secondly, ask God to empower you by faith to develop your personal devotional life. It is something He is working in you to want and to do. The early disciples sensed this. David and other saints of old sensed this. They responded to His working in their lives by meeting with God. What does meeting with God look like? In the next chapter I will walk you through a biblical explanation of the devotional life.

PART ONE
Biblical Devotions

1

THE DEVOTIONAL LIFE

Every believer needs a Devotional Transformation. If this sounds strange to you ask yourself a few questions: "Have you sensed a desire to talk with God?" "How did you learn to spend time with God?" "Was it taught to you or have you just invented a way to do it?" "Where in God's Word would you go to teach this practice to others?" "Is it optional or expected?" "Can you explain it to others?" "Is it something you do out of duty or delight?" "Who initiates the devotional life?" "How is God involved?" "How are you to be involved?" "Who sustains the practice of it?" "What is the goal of spending time with God?" "Is there a goal for having a devotional life?" "How do you know?"

How you answer these questions reveals much about what you think and do or maybe don't do. But these answers are important because this is the foundation for all biblical transformation.

In Luke 11:1, after Jesus had finished praying, one of His disciples asked, "Lord, teach us to pray just as John also taught his disciples." As the early disciples watched Jesus make time for God they caught the priority of prayer (Mark 1:35-39; Luke 5:16; 11:1). It was only a matter of time before the disciples would ask Jesus to explain what they saw Him doing. Interestingly, the devotional life of prayer is the only spiritual life skill that

His Heart, My Heart – Devotional Transformation

the first century disciples ever asked Jesus to teach them (Luke 11:1)!

Recent studies have demonstrated the value of engaging in this spiritual life skill for maintaining a vital relationship with God, overcoming obstacles to spiritual growth, moving from a self-focus to an others-focus, and aligning one's life with God's by developing a heart that beats after God's heart.[3] However, before these benefits can be realized the devotional life of prayer needs to be explained so it can be practiced.

Two points you don't want to miss here. First, prayer is the devotional life. When we look to see how Jesus spent time with God it is always explained as prayer. Second, while the **importance** of the Devotional Life can be **caught**, the **practice** of it must be **taught**. And here is the crux of the matter and why the ministry of **His Heart, My Heart Transformations** exists and begins with Devotional Transformation – every believer needs a Devotional Transformation to know biblically how it is that the devotional life is prayer as well as begin, re-boot or re-tool their practice of it; and properly pass it on to others.

Prayer, what it is and how to do it, stands as the focus of the Sermon on the Mount in Matthew 5-7.[4] Lanier

---

[3]George Barna, *Growing true disciples* (Colorado Springs, CO: WaterBrook Press, 2001); G. L. Hawkins and C. Parkinson, *Reveal: Where are you?* (Barrington, IL: Willow Creek, 2007), 48; G. L. Hawkins and C. Parkinson, *Follow Me: What's next for you?* (Barrington, IL: Willow Creek, 2008), 83-102; G. L. Hawkins and C. Parkinson, *Move: What 1,000 churches reveal about spiritual growth.* (Barrington, IL: Willow Creek, 2011), 155,181; Mike Parrott, "*His Heart, My Heart: The role of the devotional life in the discipleship process.*" (Unpublished doctoral dissertation, Gordon-Conwell Theological Seminary, Charlotte, NC. 2010).

[4]C. S. Keener, *The Gospel of Matthew: A socio-rhetorical commentary.* (Grand Rapids, MI: Eerdmans, 2009), 206; M. Nygaard, "*Prayer in the Gospels: A theological exegesis of the*

The Devotional Life

notes that "the Lord's prayer presents not only a model prayer, but a summary of Jesus' priorities embodied in a pattern for all true prayer."[5] Since Tertullian – the first extant commentary on this prayer about 200 AD – it has been understood as two sets of three petitions or six petitions with the first set relating to God and the second set relating to man.[6] Martin says, 'Lord's Prayer displays a highly poetic form characterized by the recurring use throughout of multiple coordinated figures of speech and thought".[7] In this passage two tri-cola – two sets of three petitions where each set of three is one tri-cola – are found together. The presence of a tri-cola is a sure sign of poetry. And when there are two tri-colas standing together, like there are here, it is not uncommon to find a relationship between the two sets of petitions.[8] Martin notes that the second tri-cola "mirrors" the first tri-cola.[9] Others have applied this to the Disciple's Prayer

ideal prayer" in *Biblical Interpretation Series, Vol. 144.* Anderson, P. & Sherwood, Y. (ed.). (Leiden; Boston, MA: Brill, 2012), 30.

[5] D. E. Lanier, *"The Lord's prayer: Matthew 6:9-13 – A thematic and semantic-structural analysis."* in *Criswell Theological Review 6.1.* (Wake Forest, NC: Southern Baptist Theological Seminary, 1992), 61.

[6] C. S. Keener, *The Gospel of Matthew,* 218-221; John Calvin, *Institutes of the Christian religion. Vol. 2. John T. McNeill (ed.).* (Philadelphia, PA: Westminster Press, 1975), 898; K. W. Stevenson, *Abba Father – Understanding and using the Lord's Prayer.* (Harrisburg, PA: Morehouse Publishing, 2004), 3, 28-32, 222.

[7] M. W. Martin, *"The poetry of the Lord's prayer: A study in poetic device."* in the *Journal of Biblical Literature.* 134(2), 2015, 371. doi: http://dx.doi.org/10.15699/jbl.1342.2015.2804

[8] S. P. Stocks, *"The function of the tricolon in the Psalms of Ascents"* Retrieved on October 9, 2014 from https://www.escholar.manchester.ac.uk/api/datastream?publicationP id=uk-ac-manscw:119691&datastreamId=FULL-TEXT.PDF. 81.

[9] M. W. Martin, *"The poetry of the Lord's prayer",* 370.

suggesting an A,B,C//A'B'C' relationship.[10]

These insights into this prayer are important to our understanding of it because, based upon Watson, "Appreciation of poetic technique can provide crucial clues to the correct interpretation of passages in verse."[11] Berkeley Mickelsen agrees noting that, "The literary form by which a writer conveys his ideas influences the meaning that they have upon a reader. If we ignore the form, we cannot accurately understand the meaning."[12] Here is another critical point that must not be missed: you can't properly apply a misunderstood text.

Therefore, it is critical to see clearly the structure of this text as the author intended to write it. Matthew 6:9-13 is to be understood as two parallel tricolas forming an A,B,C//A'B'C' pattern – as pictured in Figure 1. The increasing size of the double arrow in the diagram is also meant to identify a synthetic development between each line that develops upward from line to line.[13]

---

[10]C. Day, *"The Lord's prayer: A Hebrew reconstruction based on Hebrew prayers found in the Synagogue; Conspectus, Vol. 7.* (South African Theological Seminary, 2009), 27; Mike Parrott, *"His Heart, My Heart,"* 40-45; K. W. Stevenson, *Abba Father*, 36.

[11]W. G. E. Watson, *Traditional texhniques in classical Hebrew verse* (Sheffield, UK: Sheffield Academic Press, 1994), 18.

[12]A. Berkley Mickelsen, *Interpreting the Bible* (Grand Rapids, MI: Eerdmans, 1963), 44.

[13]R. Meynet, *"1998 Rhetorical Analysis: An introduction to biblical rhetoric."* in *JSOT Sup 256.* (Sheffield, UK: Sheffield Academic Press, 1998), 224-229.

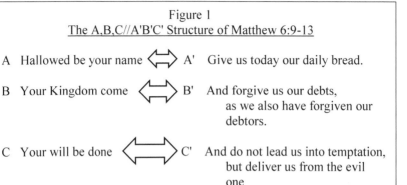

Figure 1
The A,B,C//A'B'C' Structure of Matthew 6:9-13

A Hallowed be your name ⟺ A' Give us today our daily bread.

B Your Kingdom come ⟺ B' And forgive us our debts, as we also have forgiven our debtors.

C Your will be done ⟺ C' And do not lead us into temptation, but deliver us from the evil one

Jesus' training on prayer defines the devotional life, what it is and what it intends to promote and accomplish in the life of a believer. Note that it begins in a private place free of distractions (Matthew 6:6). It is the cry of a loving relationship between God and a believer that is prompted by the work of the Holy Spirit crying "Abba, Father" (Galatians 4:6). The Holy Spirit Himself, in residence in the disciple (believer), draws him or her into relationship and communication with God for God – note it is the Holy Spirit that prompts the start of the devotional life and sustains it (cf. Jude 20).

As a believer addresses God as Father he or she then focuses upon God and His purposes by reading His Word and telling God who He is and what He does (Honoring His Name). Next the disciple discovers from God's Word what His kingdom is like and desires it to come (Your Kingdom Come), and third, the disciple discovers God's will from God's Word and wants it to be done (Your Will Be Done).

In the second set of petitions, what a believer needs to accomplish all of this is addressed: physical provisions, forgiveness, and deliverance from the flesh and the devil. In teaching prayer, the connections between God and His purposes need to be explained in relationship to what man needs to follow Him (Figure 2). In other words, trusting God for who He is leads to resting in His provisions for one's physical bodies. Confessing where we don't measure up to His Kingdom standards provides

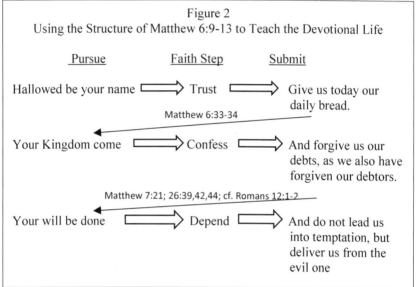

Figure 2
Using the Structure of Matthew 6:9-13 to Teach the Devotional Life

forgiveness from Him along with the need for forgiveness among one another in the Kingdom community. Dependence upon the power of the Spirit to do God's will and overcome all obstacles is the final step (cf. Ephesians 5:15-21).

Therefore, the provisions of physical resources, forgiveness, and deliverance are for the purpose of faithfully pursuing God's name, reign, and will on earth here and now. It is during this pursuit of God and His will that the believer needs physical resources, forgiveness, and deliverance that only God supplies.

Here is the very heart of prayer – to align the believer's heart with God's heart so that he or she will passionately pursue Him and His heart using His resources daily.

Time with God also involves intercession. The use of the plurals throughout this model prayer in Matthew: "Our Father," "Give us," "Forgive us," Lead us," and "Deliver us," show the heart of a true member of God's family. They desire for others what they themselves need and seek while on earth, in service and on mission for Him. While it is not wrong to use this model prayer in a corporate manner, the use of the plural phrases refer not to repeating this prayer corporately but within the context of the setting for this passage—a private place between God and a believer. Each believer must be aware of others, their needs, and ask God to work in their lives too. A practical course of action would be to pray for others about the very same things that he or she has personally discovered from God's Word like Daniel did in Daniel 9. Here Daniel was spending time in Jeremiah the prophet – most likely Jeremiah 29 since that was a letter specifically written to those in Babylon – and noticed in Jeremiah 29:10-11 that the time of Israel's captivity in Babylon was nearly finished. With this insight from God's Word Daniel prays for the people and asks God to fulfill His word. Intercessory prayer was also modelled by Jesus in John 17 and by Paul.[14]

Prayer brings us into communication with God through His Word. Developing a healthy relationship depends upon good communication.

Following the next chapter there is a 40-Day devotional that is completely based upon the Disciple's

---

[14]D. A. Carson, *A Call to Spiritual Reformation: Priorities from Paul and His Prayers* (Grand Rapids, MI: Baker Academic, 1992). It would be wise to use this resource to study these biblical prayers and use them in praying for our children and those we disciple.

Prayer as found in Matthew 6:5-13 which says,

When you pray, you are not to be like the hypocrites; for they love to stand and pray in the synagogues and on the street corners so that they may be seen by men. Truly I say to you, they have their reward in full. But you, when you pray, go into your inner room, close your door and pray to your Father who is in secret, and your Father who sees what is done in secret will reward you.

And when you are praying, do not use meaningless repetition as the Gentiles do, for they suppose that they will be heard for their many words. So do not be like them; for your Father knows what you need before you ask Him.

Pray, then, in this way:
Our Father who is in heaven.
Hallowed be Your name.
Your kingdom come.
Your will be done.
On earth as it is in heaven.
Give us this day our daily bread.
And forgive us our debts, as we also have forgiven our debtors.
And do not lead us into temptation, but deliver us from evil.
For Yours is the kingdom and the power and the glory forever, Amen.

As you move through this devotional take note of the phrases and verses in italics at the start of each day. The thoughts stated there will be expanded on for that day.

Keep in mind that you are moving step by step through Matthew 6:5-15 and taking 40 days to do this. Some days you will cover an entire verse from this passage or more. However, most days you will focus upon one line or phrase or word in this passage. In those cases, since the immediate context of the passage doesn't explain these lines or phrases or words but merely expresses them and moves on, it will be necessary to use the rest of the Bible to bring to light what the author intended by using them.

As you move through this passage in the 40-day devotional, you will be learning the devotional life as Jesus taught it. Each day builds on the previous day. So, don't rush this. Only do one devotional a day. Remember: relationships take time to develop. It is a relationship. It is a journey. Enjoy it.

Finally, your devotional life will change as you grow. The next chapter will give you an idea of what to expect in your life-time devotional journey. It is just one person's devotional journey – it happens to be mine.

While every devotional journey is different we all progress through the same stages of discipleship. Therefore, while your journey with God will be unique to you it will move you through the same stages of discipleship as all other believers have experienced through the ages. As a result, there will be common lessons you can identify with or learn about before they take place.

As you read my journey, note the key truths and principles learned within each stage. Identify the things you have already experienced and those that that you haven't yet learned. Remember, every journey is different. And yet we all move towards greater Christ-likeness day by day.

2

A DEVOTIONAL JOURNEY

As I entered the outdoor amphitheater I was delighted to find that I was the first to select this location. I wanted to be able to see the entire stadium – so I sat down high up in the left corner. It was only then that I began nervously wondering if I had made the right decision.

Just a few minutes earlier I had been sitting in the first morning meeting of a Christian conference with hundreds of college students from all over Southern California when I noticed on the conference schedule something called a 'quiet time.' I had no idea what that meant and its presence on the schedule caused some restlessness within me.

I had just come to Christ two weeks earlier. Everything was new to me. I did not grow up going to a local church but I had been to a church at least three times in the first eighteen years of my life! At least those are the times I remember. Anyway, while sitting alone, I remember thinking, "I hope someone will explain what a quiet time is all about!" I was not disappointed.

At the end of the session we were told to find a place to meet with God, talk with Him, and we were given a passage of scripture to read and think about. With that information, I set out.

I decided to climb up the mountain behind the

conference center. I was looking for a good place to sit alone and think. That was when I came to the amphitheater and strategically positioned myself where I sat down.

I tried to gather my thoughts by enjoying the pleasant early October sun and gentle breeze but then noticed that I was the only one who had chosen this location! Before my own thoughts got the best of me, I was relieved to see two more students causally walk through the seats and also position themselves strategically at equal distances around the facility. Feeling a bit more at ease, now with others around but at a distance, and with all of my distractions dealt with, I began to think about God and again enjoy the beauty of creation.

There is simply nothing like sitting outside among the mountains! What a glorious experience. I must have enjoyed the view for some time because when I looked back at the others who were spending time with God they were already reading their Bibles. So, I opened my bible to the passage I had been given.

Now I did own a bible but had only read a paragraph since receiving it back in junior high school – now I was a freshman in college. As a result, I was unfamiliar with the names of the books and what the numbers before and after the two dots meant. However, somehow, I did find my way to the right text – that was a feat itself! I actually felt like I had accomplished something just by finding the right place.

Opening God's Word and hearing Him speak to me was incredibly exciting. I had no doubt that I had a relationship with Him – I longed for time with Him. I believe the passage we were told to read was John 3:1-21. I remember thinking about the "born again" phrase that is found there. Just re-telling the story here causes me to smell the pine trees, feel the cool breeze, and recall the wonder of that first time alone in God's Word! I was talking to my Creator! The wonder of it has never worn off – even today.

Towards the end of the scheduled time I noticed the adult leader who had brought me to the conference climbing up the hillside from behind some bushes just above me. As he came towards me I wondered if he had intentionally sought me out – he was taking time to get to know me so I wouldn't have been surprised but I have never asked him about it.

However, I quickly changed my thinking as he sat down beside me and asked, 'Do you understand what you are reading?' I realized that he wanted more than a simple yes or no response to his question. So, I looked again at the passage and told him what I thought it meant. His enthusiastic response gave me confidence that I had grasped the meaning of the text and it assured me that I had done what was expected in doing a "quiet time."

THE EARLY YEARS – A NEW CHRIST FOLLOWER

Beginning a new relationship, especially with someone you can't see, works best in a quiet place with as few distractions as possible. It appeared to me that the only thing I needed to do was read my Bible and pray to develop this relationship. While that was a good beginning it was only a beginning – after all this was no ordinary relationship, it was a one-on-one time with God Himself – My Creator and the Maker of all that exists!

My experience back in early October of 1970 set the stage for my understanding of spending time with God for the next few years. There were seminars I attended that went into more explanation on spending time with God. I often heard Mark 1:35 used to support this practice – this was where Jesus had risen early after a very long day to spend time with the Father. Along with this was some exhortation to spend time in God's Word noting its significance and importance from various passages like: 2 Timothy 3:16-17; Hebrews 4:12-13; John 17:17; Psalms 119:9 and others.

With more emphasis on spending time in God's Word and even studying it I found myself moving more towards making my "quiet time" a Bible study. It seemed like an obvious direction in light of all I had heard. Although spending time with God and doing personal Bible study were often taught as two separate practices I thought that they could be somehow combined! Now I am not saying here that they shouldn't be combined but my initial attempt at doing this resulted in some unintended consequences as you will see.

During my third year as a follower of Christ my daily time with God enlarged to a one-and-a-half-hour time block where I studied God's Word, made analytical charts of various bible books, and discovered new thoughts about God. My hunger for God's Word was insatiable. I loved it! However, by the fall of 1973 my life was drying up spiritually. I was missing something or should I say I had changed something.

My practice could have worked (and later will work) but before you, so to speak, "throw the baby out with the bath water" let me explain what went wrong. I still loved to spend time in God's Word! I was seeing new thoughts about Him and His ways every day! So, why was my spiritual life shriveling up inside? It didn't make sense to me.

Just before December of 1973 God taught me the most significant truth about the devotional life – it was produced by the Spirit of God. My problem? I had begun to take it over! It was becoming more about me! I had lost the joy of building a relationship with God and letting Him talk.

Slowly my time with God had become something I had

to do, something to check off my list, something that I did each day. I had chosen the gaining of new information about God and His ways – head knowledge – over a growing relationship with God – heart knowledge or relational knowledge that transformed my whole life. My spiritual life had dried up because I wasn't aligning my life with His. I was gaining head knowledge – which is needed – but it wasn't moving the eighteen inches from my head to my heart to transform my life. It was sitting in my head as just information! It was growing stagnant there too.

What did I need? I needed God's Spirit to control my life as Paul talks about in Ephesians 5:17-18,

> So then do not be foolish, but understand what the will of the Lord is. And do not get drunk with wine, for that is dissipation, but be filled with the Spirit.

I needed to live my life by faith.

Knowing God's will and doing it is a matter of faith. I was missing the fact that the devotional life is a product of God's Spirit working in a believer's life. I was hearing Him cry out within me, "Abba, Father" and I was coming into His presence but only to learn something new. It had become all about gathering new information!

Now, it is true, my personality strength was being blessed – I enjoy thinking as God has wired my personality that way. Although all of us are a personality blend of thinking, feeling, choosing, and acting one of these tends to be more dominate than the other. For me the area of "thinking" tends to dominate. As a result, it is easy to make being personally blessed the devotional goal. I am not saying that God doesn't want to give us new thoughts to think, or make us feel close to Him, or even direct us to an action to do. God wants to change our thinking, feeling, choosing, and doing. But to stop here, to make me and being personally blessed the focus of my time with God was drying up my life. It was getting off at an exit before reaching the true goal of the devotional life and it was leaving me unprepared for the life challenges and opportunities each day.

God was producing the "desire and ability" (cf., Philippians 2:13) to spend time with Him and I was listening but I wasn't trusting Him by faith to do what He showed me. I was short-circuiting the transformational process that time with God was meant to produce! That is why my life was drying up. My life had become like the Dead Sea in Israel, truth was coming into my life but nothing was going out. I was viewing what He showed me as "optional" or something to do in the "future" but not now. I was stopping His work in me mostly by ignoring the implications of what I was seeing from His Word! It is also true that sometimes I was also "grumbling and disputing" (cf., Philippians 2:14) with Him about doing what He showed me. But the main point here is that I was trying to find joy in just the activity of discovering new truths! It was that personal blessing thing again. It was pride and that kills a relationship with God.

If this situation was going to change I had to confess this to God as wrong. I had to agree with Him I was in it for the wrong reasons and I was stopping Him from working in me!

So, I admitted this to God, but only after about three months of dryness! I honestly had not realized what had happened until later. It is hard to allow God to be God.

However, once I began to respond to Him working in me to spend time with Him, to read His Word, and to practice it, the joy returned. In fact, things changed right away – pretty much the next day! Once again it became a delight to meet with Him. My heart again longed to spend time with Him and enjoy Him. I again sought to be faithful to God and to respond to what He was asking me to do.

Acting out of duty for love of the "duty maker" is not burdensome. It becomes a delight! Psalm 40:7-8 states,

> Then I said, 'Behold, I come; in the scroll of the book it is written of me. I delight to do Your will, O my God; Your Law is within my heart.

In this passage King David is delighted in doing God's will. This text is also used of Jesus in Hebrews 10:5-7. It was again my passion too.

MINISTRY YEARS – A MATURING DISCIPLE

As I finished college and went into full-time ministry my personal time with God seemed to be doing well. I was becoming faithful to daily meet with God and seeing Him transform me. God was using it to change me and I started teaching it to others. In fact, it had become my desire to do what Ezra did: learn God's Word, practice it, and then teach others (cf. Ezra 7:10).

Teaching this skill to the high school students in my ministry was now one of my greatest joys! One example was Mike – a high school sophomore in the late 1970's in Portland, Oregon. When I first talked with him about spending daily time with God he had a number of objections. First, his alarm usually didn't wake him up and so his dad would normally have to come in and wake him up. I suggested that he make the alarm louder but he said if he turned the alarm louder it would wake up his younger brother who didn't have to get up as early as he did. So, I asked Mike to try an experiment, set his alarm for 15 minutes earlier but not louder, ask God to wake him up and not his brother, and then read his Bible and talk to God for 10 minutes before he usually got up to get ready for school. I knew that it was God who was crying out "Abba, Father" in Mike's heart and so I prayed Mike would wake up, hear God, say "yes" to Him, and begin to develop a new practice.

About three weeks later I happened to find Mike's dad in the driveway when I stopped by his home. Since I hadn't talked with his dad for a while I asked him if he had noticed any changes in his son's life. Secretly I was hoping to hear about his quiet time but I didn't want to ask him directly about it. Then he said, "Well, now when I go into Mike's room in the morning to get him up for school he is already awake reading his Bible." "Yes!" I thought to myself. That was a great start. Now I needed to help Mike focus on what was to take place as he developed his time with God.

Mike was beginning to respond to God working in his life! He would become more Christ-like in his thoughts, emotions, choices, and actions on a daily basis. He was on his way to discovering the real goal of the devotional life!

My own time with God had added journaling at this point. Maybe you have asked yourself, "Journal? What would I write about?" That actually didn't seem to be an issue for me as I could easily write for some time! Ministry creates its own challenges and being the only single male on our ministry team added a few more. There was plenty to write about and process through. Perhaps that was the most valuable part of what I first learned about journaling was it allowed me to express my thoughts so I could see what I was really thinking and it helped me to begin to work through my own issues. Later, it would allow me also to look back and see clearly how God was causing me to grow as well as giving me direction in life.

However, as I added journaling to my time with God I noticed that some days I barely spent any time in God's word! In fact, I could find myself musing over my thoughts for forty-five minutes or more and then realize I only had five minutes left before I needed to get going for the day.

Eventually this seemed out of balance. What do I mean here? You probably know that the Psalms are filled with examples from David's life where He spent time with God telling Him his true feelings. Psalm 72 says, "The prayers of David the son of Jesse are ended." The Psalms are prayers, individual and group times with God. Martin Luther believed the Psalms to be a school of prayer. He wrote:

> The Christian can learn to pray in the psalter, for here he can hear how the saints talk with God. The number of moods which are expressed here, joy and suffering, hope and care, make it possible for every Christian to find himself in it, and to pray with the psalms.[15]

The Psalms can be divided into two groups: Praise and Lament. The Psalms of Praise speak of life being good while the Psalms of Lament speak of life being tough. In my journaling, I had been focusing on life being tough. But what I had not known is that every "Life is Tough" psalm ended with a vow to praise or an actual shout of praise to God.[16]

I was experiencing a lot of things that I felt were tough at the time and so I felt my practice was biblical until I discovered this truth about the "Life is Tough" psalms.

---

[15] Ronald Barclay Allen, *Praise! A Matter of Life and Breath* (Nashville, TN: Thomas Nelson Publishers, 1980), 24.
[16] Ibid., 38.

Not getting time in God's Word to get His perspective was often missing from my time with Him. And this was a problem.

On the days when I did get to God's Word I noticed that just getting God's perspective on my complaints, concerns, issues, and problems helped me more than all my writing about them. So, I thought, maybe I should start with God's Word first then write about my feelings.

So, I adjusted my time with God and something radically changed. I wasn't spending all my time with God complaining about my situation. Instead, all my complaints, concerns, issues, and problems seemed to fade into the distance after reading God's Word first! I was now journaling only briefly about my feelings and focusing on what God's Word said!

This shouldn't have been a surprise to me since I knew that Daniel 9 was a great passage that could be used to teach the devotional life. In this passage Daniel is reading in the book of Jeremiah the prophet for His time with God. He starts with God's Word and that leads into prayer. So, I began to start with God's Word first. Even when I was feeling challenged I would find a Psalm that expressed how I felt and spend time in it.

Over the next few years as I continued this practice of reading God's Word, praising His name, and then talking about my concerns with Him I still wanted to understand more about the devotional life. I began to think about some deeper questions about it like, "Should I be telling God all my issues since He already knows them?" After all, He is God, He designed me, and according to Psalm 139 He knows my thoughts before I even process through them! My other questions were: "What is the devotional life?" "Where is it talked about in Scripture?" "How did Jesus spend time with God?"

I was convinced that personal time with God was the single key to growth as a follower of Christ. My own

A Devotional Journey

previous experience had certainly demonstrated this, but my questions lingered. It wasn't that I thought that what I was doing was wrong. I simply wondered if there was more to it. I wanted to explore it as fully as possible. I was also attending seminary during this time and that intensified my questions and study of God's Word.

As I began hearing others teach about spiritual disciplines that would only compound my questions as it seemed that time with God was slipping into just one spiritual practice among many. This compelled me even more to discover the biblical basis for it. I was concerned that the practice was now becoming the product of man's invention rather than what God intended His disciples to do and what He was driving them towards. This was something I reacted to.

So, I started with the basics, "Where is time with God found in God's Word?" "When others spent time with God what did they do?" You may think that these questions had already been resolved earlier in my walk with God. And you would be right – as I quickly knew the answers to my questions but it would be a few more years before I would understand the real depth and significance of my answers!

All you have to do is think about Mark 1:35-37 and ask yourself what was Jesus doing when He spent time with God? This passage says,

> In the early morning, while it was still dark, Jesus got up, left the house, and went away to a secluded place, and was praying there. Simon and his companions searched for Him; they found Him, and said to Him, "Everyone is looking for You."

I have to admit that I have always been taken back by what Mark records here because I really expected Peter

51

(Simon) to say, "What are you doing out here by yourself?" But that isn't what he says. Instead of trying to discover what Jesus was doing and why he is doing it, he is concerned that Jesus isn't with him and the others. Really Peter? Is it all about you?

Jesus doesn't address this apparent attitude here. Instead, he tells Peter and the others that they are to stay on mission and go to other cities. You should be asking here, "How did Jesus know that was the next step in the plan?" I think He got His orders during his time with God that Peter just interrupted. But what was Jesus doing out in the wilderness all alone? Did you catch it? He was praying.

Does that mean that prayer is how you spend time with God? My understanding of prayer at this point in my walk with God would not have been defined this way. In fact, I had only heard prayer defined in terms of coming to God with our own personal requests or requesting things for others. Could the issue be my understanding of "prayer?"

My first thoughts instantly turned towards the Psalms and then to Jesus' teaching on prayer in the Sermon on the Mount – Matthew 6:5-15. A quick read of Jesus' explanation of prayer in Matthew 6 certainly sounds a lot like the devotional life. In fact, I believe that it is the key spiritual discipline for every believer; even the Grand Central Station for every spiritual discipline. But I would not grasp all the depth of this for a few more years.

I began to read everything I could on prayer at this point. I found the works of E. M. Bounds and George Muller to be particularly inspiring. But it wouldn't be until I began an in-depth study of Matthew 6:5-15 that I would finally answer all my questions about the devotional life.

FRUITFUL MINISTRY YEARS – A MULTIPLYING DISCIPLE

In the fall of 1984 my life seemed hopeful. My wife and I had three children and were expecting a fourth. We had the hope of a new exciting change in ministry. We had a home we were buying and we couldn't have been more excited about our future. At the end of December all of this changed. In a matter of two weeks our home sold since we expected to move to a new ministry location, our expected child passed away in the womb at 20 weeks, and our hope for a new ministry vanished. Suddenly we had no home, no ministry change, and the loss of a child. We would end up staying in our current ministry but found ourselves without a stable place to live for the next three months and found ourselves going slowly through the grief process. It honestly felt like a Job experience.

However, through difficult times God matures us (James 1:2-4) or demonstrates our maturity and moves us towards living the rest of our lives for His will (I Peter 4:1-2). This was a unique time for me to talk with God using the Psalms. I found my thoughts expressed well there.

As I worked through various Psalms I found the words of Psalm 73:25-28 to express my heart well,

> Whom have I in heaven but You?
> And besides You, I desire nothing on earth.
> My flesh and my heart may fail,
> But God is the strength of my heart and my portion forever.
> For, behold, those who are far from You will perish;
> You have destroyed all those who are unfaithful

53

to You.

But as for me, the nearness of God is my good;
I have made the Lord God my refuge, That I may
tell of all Your works.

From this point on my devotional life became focused
on living to do God's will no matter what it might cost me.
My journaling became focused on understanding and
doing God's word. Not that it wasn't like this before but
now there was a different sense of abandonment to Him
and His will. This would show itself over the next years
in fruitful ministry.

How fruitful? While my ministry before this time saw
others come to Christ and become reproducers of the
faith, it continued to average between 20-35 students.
Please note that numbers don't tell you everything that is
happening but when you read the book of Acts even God
uses numbers to give you a sense of how He is working!

Then, from 1985 to 1990, I was able to start a new
ministry from scratch and see God grow it from 0 to 64
students! In 1990, I would move to another location and
see Him grow my ministry from a handful to over 100
students after several years. Early in the 1990's we had a
team of 12 full-time youth workers and 35 volunteers
working with students from 17 different schools! During
this time, we were giving 14,000 students on a yearly
basis the opportunity to hear the gospel.

Through all these years I was also able to be involved
in overseas short-term mission projects and lead many of
them to places like: Paris, Manila, Moscow, Leningrad,
Budapest, Jerusalem, Siberia, Quito, Nairobi and
Kampala. These two-week and sometimes 30-day
projects would happen on the average of one every other
year which continues to be the pattern. A number of
these projects would return to the same location again.
Some projects had as few as 10 like Kampala, Uganda in

2002 but we would still see nearly 1,000 students come to Christ. Other projects were large like Manila, Philippines in 1990 where we had 420! I didn't lead that one but in 1992 the project I lead to Moscow, Russia would have 72. On that project, we would share the gospel with 14,000 students in 40 different schools in just two weeks and see 2,500 indicate a first-time decision for Christ!

These were incredibly fruitful ministry years! And they haven't ended. During my time in full-time teaching at a Christian University, I was still able to invest in a worldwide ministry. This includes projects to Quito (2005), Nairobi and Kampala (2012), and then again to Kampala (2014) where I was able to lead a team of 10 back to Africa and see over 1,200 decisions for Christ after sharing the gospel with over 5,500 students over the course of 30 days.

With the start of my new ministry, **His Heart, My Heart Transformations**, I have already had hundreds of adults complete the *His Heart, My Heart – Devotional Transformation* devotional on devotions and see their lives transformed. Also, hundreds have completed my **Shepherd Leadership Transformational Training** and learned how to lead others through all the stages of discipleship. Those who did this training as Mature or Multiplying Disciples were able to see their own ministry both one-on-one and in small groups rapidly grow. Perhaps by 2018 I will be able to say that thousands have been trained.

I could go on and describe my church ministry since 1980 too: leadership roles, discipleship, teaching, and preaching, but you get the idea. After my heart became completely committed to doing His will and continues to do it God has blessed everything. This all starts with daily time with God. My daily devotional life has truly kept me on track. And it is all *His Story*!

A DISCIPLE'S DEVOTIONAL LIFE

Learning the devotional life is a journey. There may be twists and turns in your journey now! There may be things you need to change or to straighten out an already crooked or confusing practice. And as you adjust what you do there are a number of truths you should keep in mind.

Spirit Prompted

Time with God is clearly God prompted! Just remember that it is indeed God who cries out "Abba, Father" in your life! This is not a quiet voice either. You know you are being drawn into a relationship with Him. Say "yes" to Him! Don't drown it out with distractions.

Transformational

God is clearly using this practice to change your life from the inside out. Time with God will transform your thoughts, feelings, choices, and actions. Spending time in God's Word allows you to learn new truths about God, His ways and grow. It will also draw you close to Him so you feel closer. It will also move you to act in faith on what He wants you to do. You will be personally benefited but don't make it the goal. He is the goal.

Trust God to renew your thoughts with His thoughts from His Word. Let Him change your emotions towards loving what He loves and hating what He hates. Make new choices by wanting the best, selecting the best and doing the best for yourself and others. Depend upon His power to act more like Christ in both word and deed by faith. God will make you like Jesus as you daily spend time with Him.

God Focused

All of this is designed by God to provide the foundation for the ultimate goal of personal time with God. What is the "ultimate goal?" As you daily follow Christ you are being totally transformed from the inside out so that your heart begins to beat with a heart after His heart. In other words, you are arriving at what Paul calls the, "riches of the glory of His inheritance in the saints" (Eph. 1:18b). Notice here that God gets something by inheriting you as His child! What is it? He gets another vessel to display Himself through to His glory! He gets a life with a heart that beats with His heart. Therefore, let His Heart become Your Heart.

To have a heart that is like His heart means that God has redeemed and sanctified vessels of glory so that they will reflect Him and His passion in this world here and now just like Jesus did when He walked among mankind in the flesh! Just as the Father sent the Son so the Son has sent us. He chose not to take believers out of this world, nor did He want them to be of this world, but instead He wanted them to be in it (John 17:15-18). That is significant. Believers are here to engage this world as God's own Son engaged it by doing the Father's will for His glory!

Progressive

Your time with God will move through a number of stages. I believe there are three: personal benefit focused, others focused, and His will focused. You should be able to clearly identify these three from my own devotional story above! If you missed this just scan back over the titles to the sections and you will see the stages.

Getting perspective on what is happening in this world and how we engage it begins in our personal time with God – the devotional life. A sermon by John Eliot, a Puritan back in the seventeenth century, notes the value of spending time with God:

> In the morning, if we ask, "Where am I to be to-day?" our souls must answer, "In heaven." In the evening, if we ask, "Where have I been to-day?" our souls may answer, "In heaven." If thou art a believer, thou art no stranger to heaven while thou livest; and when thou diest,
> heaven will be no strange place to thee; no, thou hast been there a thousand times before.[17]

While some think that a person who is so heavenly minded will be of no earthly good it turns out that the exact opposite is true: you will never be of any earthly good until you are heavenly minded. Only with His perspective will a believer know what is needed in this world here and now. Only by daily checking in with our Lord and moment by moment walking with Him will we act as He did. Only as we spend time with God will we be personally transformed and be a transforming influence for Him and His purposes in this world.

So, this is the devotional life. How are you doing in reaching the ultimate goal? It is all a God thing! If you simply spend time with God to appear spiritual or to check it off a list of things to do it will not transform you or this world. "Should I not spend time with God because

---

[17] Charles E. Hambrick-Stowe *The Practice of Piety, Puritan Devotional Disciplines in Seventeenth-Century New England* (Chapel Hill, NC: The University of North Carolina Press, 1982), xvi.

my attitude isn't right?" Absolutely not! That is like saying, "Should I wait until I feel like it to love my mate." No, you should love your mate – if you are married. And you should love God and spend time with Him because He is drawing you to Himself crying, "Abba, Father." To not respond is wrong. If you love the "duty maker" – God – then out of love for Him you should act in faith. If you continue to treat time with God as a "duty" you will always find yourself failing due to the corruption that is still in you from the sin nature. If you live in "grace" not "law" you will delight to spend time with Him. If your attitude is different give it to Him. Ask Him to change your will to a "want to". If you respond to the Holy Spirit working in your life you will delight to do His will.

So, how should you proceed? Before beginning this devotional on devotions think about who is controlling your life? Is it God or self? Are you depending upon Him to do what He has designed for you to do?

Making sure you are rightly related to the work of God in your life through the Holy Spirit is a daily, moment by moment, and decision by decision practice if you are going to see real spiritual growth in your life. Are you ready to begin developing the ultimate relationship of a lifetime? Do you sense the "cry of relationship" within you that draws you into wanting to talk with God? Are you ready for a deep, intimate, eternal, relationship with the living God Himself?

Day One of the devotional on devotions begins now. Remember, only do one devotional a day as a relationship takes time to develop. Deal with any legalistic resistance or rebellion towards these by confessing this to God and moving through this to delight. Do not grieve or quench His work in your life. Joyfully spend time with Him out of delight.

If you aren't there yet don't wait until you "feel" like it as you will never "naturally" feel like it. Only by responding to God's supernatural work in your life to desire and do His word will you ever "feel" like it. So, push through the "duty" mentality and arrive at the "delight" of building an eternal, supernatural relationship with your loving Father who cares about you and has great things in store for you.

Come enjoy the relational experience, life transforming adventure, and culturally impacting journey. Come discover the daily joy of a heart that beats for Him and His heart. Let the adventure begin!

PART TWO

The 40-Day Devotional
on Devotions

"Humble yourself and pray."
—2 Chronicles 7:14a

DAY ONE – HIGHEST PRIORITY

When you pray...
—Matthew 6:5

Then men began to call upon the name of the Lord.
—Genesis 4:26b

And in the early morning, while it was still dark, He arose and went out, and departed to a lonely place, and was praying there.
—Mark 1:35

Give ear, O Lord, to my prayer; and give heed to the voice of my supplications! In the day of my trouble I shall call upon Thee, for Thou wilt answer me. There is no one like Thee among the gods, O Lord; nor are there any works like Thine. All nations whom Thou hast made shall come and worship before Thee, O Lord; and they shall glorify Thy name, for Thou art great and doest wondrous deeds; Thou alone art God.
—Psalm 86:6-10

Approach God today by telling Him who He is. Complete this phase a number of times, "Lord, you are _____" and each time you say it fill in how you see Him. Use the verses in italics above to direct your thoughts. If you need more help see the light grey options below. Take a couple of minutes to do this now and then continue with this day's devotional on the next page.

Lord you are...
the one I call out to,
the one who hears,
my help in trouble,
like none other,
great,
the doer of wondrous deeds,
God alone.

Now simply ask Him to speak to you. Turn to Mark 1:29-39 read it and answer the following questions:

What was this day like for Jesus?

What did He do the next morning?

What word is used to describe His time meeting with God?

When you hear this word what comes to mind?
   Jot a few thoughts here:

Often the term "prayer" brings to our minds a time when we take our requests before God. In scripture, however, it is more than that, it is the term used to describe the devotional life. If you want to know how to spend time with God you need to learn how to pray. In fact, this is the only skill that the disciples ever asked Jesus to teach them (Luke 11:1). While Jesus had taught them how to pray in the Sermon of the Mount it is Luke who records that it wasn't until the disciples wanted to learn to pray that He taught the same thing again. The point here is that we don't tend to learn new things until we want to and sometimes it just takes more than one lesson to really get it.

Are you ready to learn to pray? Why or why not?

What resistance do you have towards doing this?

How should you deal with any resistance in light of what you read in the Introduction? (If you didn't read the Introduction yet you need to go back and do so now before you continue this devotional.)

In the Sermon on the Mount, Matthew 6:5, Jesus starts this discussion about prayer with the phrase, "And when you pray." As you think about the term "when" how do you understand it? Which of these options do you think the text has in mind here?

1. "If you ever do this."
2. "If you want to do this someday."
3. "Because you should do this."
4. "Because you will do this."
5. "Because you will repeatedly want to do this."

The term used for "when" here is "ὅταν."
(Technically, the term is a temporal adverb used with the verb "pray" which is in a present tense subjunctive mood. What that means is that this is the normal construction for something that is often repeated or a possible action in the present or future.)

Do you think Jesus is teaching this as something Optional or Expected? Why?

(Note: Did you consider that the Holy Spirit is moving you into communication with God as your Father in your response? Would this change what you wrote above? If so, how?)

65

Did the overall context of this passage help you decide? How?

Since prayer is something expected of a true believer and that he or she will want to do, it would be good to know what it is and how to do it.

Ask God to teach you how to spend time with Him even if you have spent time with Him for years. Ask Him to teach you to pray or to teach you afresh how to pray. Take a minute and tell Him now.

Think through those you know who need to learn how to pray or spend time with God. Think through those who need to say "yes" to God prompting them to draw close to Him. Ask God to teach them to pray and respond to God in his or her life. Be specific here. Who are you praying will learn this too? List them below:

DAY TWO – NOT A PERFORMANCE

"When you pray, you are not to be like the hypocrites; for they love to stand and pray in the synagogues and on the street corners so that they may be seen by men. Truly I say to you, they have their reward in full."

—Matthew 6:5

"And He also told this parable to some people who trusted in themselves that they were righteous, and viewed others with contempt: 'Two men went up into the temple to pray, one a Pharisee and the other a tax collector. The Pharisee stood and was praying this to himself: 'God, I thank You that I am not like other people: swindlers, unjust, adulterers, or even like this tax collector. I fast twice a week; I pay tithes of all that I get.' But the tax collector, standing some distance away was even unwilling to lift up his eyes to heaven, but was beating his breast saying, 'God, be merciful to me, the sinner!' I tell you, this man went to his house justified rather than the other; for everyone who exalts himself will be humbled, but he who humbles himself will be exalted."

—Luke 18:9-14

As you begin time with God today use the verses above to again tell Him who He is and what He does. Take a couple of minutes to reflect on these verses and again use the phrase, "Lord you are _____ " to help guide your thoughts. If you need further guidance see the light grey thoughts here:

> Lord you are...
> the one I humbly bow before,
> the God of mercy,
> my righteousness,
> the one who justifies.

Yesterday you discovered that the phrase "when you pray" meant that as a believer you will repeatedly pray. Since we will do this often we should ask, "How should we do it?" Jesus begins by first stating how it should not be done.

From Matthew 6:5, how should it not be done?

Why is it not to be done like the hypocrites?

The term 'hypocrite' comes from the Greek theater where a performer would put on a mask in order to play a part. He or she would pretend to be someone they were not. Why is Jesus saying here that a believer should not be like a hypocrite when he or she prays?

Are we praying to be seen by men or God? What is the difference?

As you meet with God today turn to Isaiah 6:1-7.

What is God like in verses 1-4?

Take a minute and tell God who He is based on this passage. Again, use the phrase, "Lord you are _____" and fill in the blank using how He is described here in Isaiah 6:1-4.

When we see God as He really is how should we respond according to Isaiah 6:5?

In light of this, look back at the way the Pharisee approached God in Luke 18:9-14 at the start of this day's devotional, did this Pharisee grasp who God is? Why or why not?

From the response of the sinner in Luke 18:9-14 and the response of Isaiah in Isaiah 6:5, how should we respond when we really see God?

Humility is the proper response before God. When we see God as He truly is we realize we cannot justify ourselves before Him. We are "ruined" or "undone" as Isaiah 6:5 says. But it is God who forgives and justifies us through His graciousness. He forgives us. Take a minute and ask God to search your heart for anything that isn't pleasing to Him. Whatever comes to mind, do not ignore it or rationalize it away. The fact that it came to your mind when you asked Him to search your heart is evidence of the Holy Spirit identifying something you need to confess to God. Agree that it is wrong and ask Him for power to take a 180° turn away from this and follow God's way. Take a minute to do this and then read the next passage.

I John 1:9 says, "If we confess our sins, He is faithful and righteous to forgive us our sins and to cleanse us from all unrighteousness." Take a moment and thank God for forgiving you.

Now think of others who need to learn what you learned today. Who do you know who needs humility as they come into God's presence to speak with Him?

Who do you know who needs to approach God more reverently like Isaiah?

Who do you know who needs God's forgiveness?

Ask God to bring them to the point of recognizing their sin, realizing their need, confessing their sin, and experiencing God's love and forgiveness. Who comes to mind? List them below. Don't forget to include yourself.

DAY THREE – A QUIET PLACE

*"When you pray, go into your inner room, close your door
and pray to your Father who is in secret, and your Father
who sees what is done in secret will reward you."*
—Matthew 6:6

"For this reason I bow my knees before the Father,...
—Ephesians 3:14

Start this time by telling God who He is and what He
does. Use the above verses to get you started. You can
use the phrase, "Lord you are _____" again if that is
helping you. Again, see the light grey ideas below if you
need them:

> Lord you are...
> my Father,
> the one who sees me,
> the one I bow before,
> the one who rewards me.

In Matthew 6:6 we discover one of the positive things
to do as we pray. From this passage, how should we
pray? (List several items from this verse)

In this verse, we discover that we are to pray to our
Father who is in secret. When you started your time with
God today did you tell Him that He was your Father?
How do you feel about Him being your Father? Can you
praise Him that He is your Father? Take a minute and
do so if you can.

Perhaps you have not had a father figure in your life or you have had a very difficult experience with your earthly father. The absence or dysfunctional nature of your father has most likely affected your ability to embrace God as your heavenly Father. What you want to see here is that your heavenly Father is everything that you should have had as a father. He is the Father of the fatherless. He is the perfect Father who doesn't change, is always there, and loves you. Treating God as Father may take some time for you to embrace but keep working on replacing wrong thoughts about your father or being a father with God's Word about what a real Father is like and start thanking Him for who He is and what He does.

Also in this verse, you find that you are to meet with the Father in private. What do the following passages also suggest about where we should meet with God?

> Luke 22:39-46 –
> Daniel 6:10 –
> Mark 1:35 –

These passages note the importance of praying in private. It should be a place free of distractions. It should be a place where you would feel comfortable to take on any posture: kneeling, lying prostrate on the floor, sitting in a chair with raised hands to God, or any other posture. Do you have a private place to meet with God? If not, ask God to show you a place you can be with Him in private. Where will you meet with Him?

According to Mark 1:36-37 what can happen if we don't have a private place?

What distracts you from spending time with God?

What could you do to minimize or eliminate these distractions?

Where can you meet with God without distractions?

What discipline will you have to apply to your life to maintain a proper place to meet with God?

Ask God to help you maintain a private place to meet regularly with Him.

Pray for those you know who are struggling with calling God their Father. Also, pray for those who need a more suitable place to meet with God. Pray they will make this a priority and arrange their lives to do it.

Note: Are you seeing some patterns developing that explains how to spend daily time with God? Can you identify some of them even though based on just your first few days of doing this? List what you think you see and talk with your discipler/mentor or small group leader about what you think you see at this point.

DAY FOUR – NOT A QUIET TIME

"My lips will praise You."
—Psalm 63:3b

"Give ear to my prayer, O God;
And do not hide Yourself from my supplication."
—Psalm 55:1

"Then David the king went in and sat before the Lord, and he said, ..."
—2 Samuel 7:18a

"Now it can about, as she continued praying before the Lord, that Eli was watching her mouth. As for Hannah, she was speaking in her heart, only her lips were moving, but her voice was not heard."
—I Samuel 1:12-13a

"Jesus spoke these things; and lifting up His eyes to heaven, He said, ..."
—John 17:1a

"When you are praying, do not use meaningless repetition as the Gentiles do, for they suppose that they will be heard for their many words."
—Matthew 6:7

Begin today by reading the above verses and using them to praise God. Praise God by specifically telling Him who He is and what He does. Take a minute and do this now.

As you read all the verses above for today's time with God, does it seem that prayer is to be done silently in your heart or spoken out loud to God? Did you praise God silently or out loud just now? Why did you do it the way you did?

Since speaking our prayer out loud appears to be the normal way to pray, does this make it more important that you have a place away from others for prayer?

Why?

In all the verses above there is the expectation of prayer being audible – something that is heard. While Hannah's prayer is noted as being done in her heart to God, Eli appears to have expected her prayer to be able to be heard. As a result, in context, Eli misunderstands Hannah's spirit before God and supposes that she is drunk (I Samuel 13b) which she promptly denies. There are places in God's Word where we do find silent prayer: Abraham (Genesis 24:45); Nehemiah (Nehemiah 2:4); and in Isaiah 26:16. The point here is that "silent prayer" is not the norm, it is the exception.

Notice from the following verses the vocal nature of prayer:
John 11:41-44

Did you notice that in His prayer Jesus explains why He said the previous words in verses 39-40?

Jesus prays out loud for all to hear in this situation.

Have you ever prayed for all to hear?

Matthew 26:36-44

Did you notice that Jesus leaves eight of His disciples in one place to pray, then three other disciples in another place to pray, and finally Jesus moves further away and prays out loud to God the Father? Did you also notice that each group has different information about what to pray about in their different places?

Prayer is expected to be heard. Its very nature expects that what is said will be heard by God. Prayer is where you express the full extent of your heart to God. The author of the book of Hebrews says in 5:7, "In the days of His flesh, He offered up both prayers, and supplications with loud crying and tears to the One able to save Him from death, and He was heard because of His piety."

Take a minute a tell God out loud how grateful you are that He wants you to speak out loud to Him what is really on your heart.

Praise Him for who He is and what He does.

Tell Him about how you feel about speaking out loud to Him in your devotions.

Ask Him to help you develop this aspect of your time with God.

Ask God to help others develop this ability to talk out loud to God during his or her devotions.

DAY FIVE – NOT MANY WORDS

"And when you are praying, do not use meaningless repetition as the Gentiles do, for they suppose that they will be heard for their many words."
—Matthew 6:7

"Guard your steps as you go to the house of God and draw near to listen rather than to offer the sacrifice of fools; for they do not know they are doing evil. Do not be hasty in word of impulsive in thought to bring up a matter in the presence of God. For God is in heaven and you are on the earth; therefore let your words be few."
—Ecclesiastes 5:1-2

Before working through the verses above, take a minute to worship God using these verses. Tell Him who He is and where He is in your own words.

How we approach God, who we have come to believe He is, what He is like, and on what basis we believe we can come before Him and He hears us is important. As you reflect on the two passages above there are two issues that need to be addressed. First, coming to God with the idea that we have done something to earn the right to speak with Him rather than realizing that He has done everything that is necessary for us to speak with Him. Second, that we are approaching God as He really is and not making Him into our own design – distorting His true nature and character.

In today's devotional, the first issue will be addressed and the second one will be taken up tomorrow. So, based on these verses, how can someone demonstrate through his or her actions that they misunderstand how they are to come before God and speak with Him?

You should have noticed several wrong ways people think they have the right to come to God: meaningless repetition of many words, offering the sacrifice of fools, and failure to realize that God is in heaven and we are earth bound. The idea of "meaningless repetition of many words" is not saying we can't repeat a request before God. It is also not saying that long prayers are wrong. It is saying don't meaninglessly repeat your words. Don't babble. Don't use long repetitious wording to justify yourself before God. Don't use incantations – a series of words like a magic spell. This is not how you are to approach God.

This is also the idea of offering "the sacrifice of fools". In this passage, the person misses the fact that they are sinning and that sin hasn't been dealt with and they seek to justify themselves before God with sacrifices, personal accomplishments, all in the attempt to earn God's ear and then thinking He is obligated to do what they want Him to do. Seeking to justify yourself before God will always fail.

On what basis do you have the right, privilege, to come before God and speak with Him?

If you have accepted Jesus' sacrifice on the cross as payment for your sins, confessed that Jesus is your Savior and Lord and that God raised Him from the dead – which demonstrates that Jesus' sacrifice satisfied God's anger against sin – then you have been brought into the family of God as His child (cf. John 1:12-13; Romans 10:9). As a child of God, a member of God's family, you have access to God as your Father and can confidently come before Him (cf. Hebrews 4:16).

If you have never accepted Jesus' death on the cross as payment for your own personal sins, faults, failure to live up to God's standards then it is time for you to pause here and accept Jesus as your Savior and Lord. Take a minute now and accept Him as Savior and Lord. Just talk with Him. Tell Him your need for Him and what He has done for you through Jesus' death on the cross for your sins. Thank Him for coming into your life, forgiving your sins, and beginning the great adventure of eternal life.

When you come to faith in Jesus' finished work on the cross as payment for your own sins, accepting Him as your Savior and Lord you begin eternal life. John, the apostle, records Jesus' own words about eternal life in John 17:3, "This is eternal life, that they may know You, the only true God, and Jesus Christ whom You have sent." John later writes again about this in I John 5:11-12 saying, "And the testimony is this, that God has given us eternal life, and this life is in His Son. He who has the Son has the life; he who does not have the Son of God does not have the life."

Now continue to spend time with God – your Father. Picture yourself standing in His presence. Praise Him that He possesses life forever as part of His very nature as God.

Praise God for being the author of life. He alone has always existed and always will. All those who have life – biologically and spiritually – have it because life only arises from life. For there to be living beings other than God they had to get that life from the One – triune God – Father, Son, and Holy Spirit – who eternally possesses life (cf. John 5:26; Colossians 1:15-20; Revelation 1:8). God gives eternal life to those who believe in Jesus. Praise Him.

Pray today for those you know who need life in His name. Pray for those who need to come to faith in Jesus Christ as their Savior and Lord.

DAY SIX – GOD KNOWS

"So do not be like them; for your Father knows what you need before you ask Him."
—Matthew 6:8

"For this reason I say to you, do not be worried about your life, as to what you will eat or what you will drink; nor for your body, as to what you will put on. Is not life more than food, and the body more than clothing? Look at the birds of the air, that they do not sow, nor reap nor gather into barns, and yet your heavenly Father feeds them. Are you not worth much more than they? And who of you by being worried can add a single hour to his life? And why are you worried about clothing? Observe how the lilies of the field grow; they do not toil nor do they spin, yet I say to you that not even Solomon in all his glory clothed himself like one of these. But if God so clothes the grass of the field, which is alive today and tomorrow is thrown into the furnace, will He not much more clothe you? You of little faith! Do not worry then, saying, 'What will we eat?' or 'What will we drink?' or 'What will we wear for clothing?' For the Gentiles eagerly seek all these things. But seek first His kingdom and His righteousness, and all these things will be added to you. So do not worry about tomorrow; for tomorrow will care for itself. Each day has enough trouble of its own."
—Matthew 6:25-34

Start today as before worshipping Him for who He is and what He does. Use the verses above to guide your thoughts. Write down one characteristic about who God is or what He does that captures your attention the most:

Knowing God: who He is, His nature, His character, His works, is the second issue the verses for today address. Too often God isn't embraced as He is but is

85

made into a "god" of our own design. How do the verses for today suggest God can be incorrectly viewed?

God is your Father. He knows what you need. Earlier, in Day Three, you read about how addressing God as Father can affect you. Now it is time to make sure you are developing right thoughts about God being your Father. So once again take a minute and praise Him for His care for you. Tell Him who He is. Use this format, "Father, you _____." Fill in the attribute, characteristic, quality, that describes Him. Write the words you use below:

God hears us when we pray. As we saw yesterday, we aren't to come to Him with meaningless repetition or the sacrifices of fools. We are to be authentic before Him. We are to come as family members, His children, knowing that as a Father He knows us better than we know ourselves. He desires to meet our needs and will do so. The issue is one of faith. In the passage above from Matthew Jesus chides the disciples saying, "You of little faith!" Little faith doesn't know the object of its faith very well. Therefore, it is little faith.

Considering this, do you believe what the Scriptures say about God as your Father?

Why or why not?

How can your faith grow?

Paul says in Romans 10:17, "So faith comes from hearing, and hearing by the word of Christ." In Ecclesiastes 5:1-2, from yesterday, we are told we are to come before God to listen. The only way to hear from God is to be students of His Word – the Bible. If we are going to grow in faith we must know who God is, what He is like, what He wants, and who we are and what we need. We need God's Word to know Him and His ways. Trust is best developed in a family with a shepherd leader. God Himself is our Shepherd as Psalm 23 says, "The Lord is my Shepherd." This is the way to grow in faith, develop greater trust, and have more confidence in God and His ways.

What basic needs do you need to trust God to provide for you today?

Trust God to act on your behalf by thanking Him for providing these things ahead of time. The very act of thanking Him demonstrates faith. Take a minute and thank Him that He will meet each real need you listed above.

Who do you know who needs to spend time in God's Word, believe it, and grow in his or her faith?

Who do you know who needs to believe that Father God will take care of their current real, legitimate needs?

Pray for these individuals. Pray they believe God's Word. Pray they trust God, their Father, to address each need.

DAY SEVEN – CALL HIM FATHER

*Pray, then, in this way: "Our **Father** who is in heaven, Hallowed be Your name.*
—*Matthew 6:9*

*For You are our **Father**, though Abraham does not know us and Israel does not recognize us. You, O LORD, are our **Father**, Our Redeemer from of old is Your name.*
—*Isaiah 63:16*

*But now, O LORD, You are our **Father**, We are the clay, and You our potter; And all of us are the work of Your hand.*
—*Isaiah 64:8*

According to Matthew 6:9 where is your Father?

When you are meeting with God where are you when you address Him since your Father is in heaven?

Where does Hebrews 4:16 say you are when you come to Him?

You are brought into His throne room, His Holy presence, and you call Him Father! What an incredible privilege!

Take a few moments and talk to your Father in heaven. Tell Him who He is and how you see Him in light of the verses above.

What is the difference between being able to call God your Father versus standing before God while someone else calls Him Father but not you?

How did the thought of being in God's presence motivate Paul in 2 Corinthians 5:11?

How did this motivate John in I John 1:1-4?

How should it motivate you according to what Paul says in Philippians 2:12-16 and what John says in I John 3:1-3?

Who are you according to Isaiah 64:8 at the start of this day's devotional?

How does this truth make you feel?

How should you respond in light of it?

Knowing God personally as your Father is a precious privilege. It is something we should desire for everyone. Think about those you know who don't know God as their Father. Make a list and begin praying daily for them to come to Christ (cf. Romans 10:1).

Think about those believers you know who aren't responding to being in His presence by embracing Him as Father and responding to Him as family members molded like clay by His hand. Pray they would appropriately and humbly come before God and call Him Father.

Finally, spend a few minutes thanking God for your relationship with Him and being your Father. Why not use the space here to write Him a note thanking Him?

DAY EIGHT – LIVING LIKE FAMILY

Pray, then, in this way: Our Father...
—Matthew 6:9

Father, the hour has come; glorify Thy Son, that the Son may glorify Thee, even as Thou gavest Him authority over all mankind, that to all whom Thou hast given Him, He may give eternal life. And this is eternal life, that they may know Thee, the only true God, and Jesus Christ whom Thou hast sent.
—John 17:1b-3

For even as the body is one and yet has many members, and all the members of the body, though they are many, are one body, so also is Christ. For by one Spirit we were all baptized into one body, whether Jews or Greeks, whether slaves or free, and we were all made to drink of one Spirit.
—I Corinthians 12:12-13

As you begin your time with God today ask Him to speak to you. Then turn your attention to the verses above and tell God who His is and what He does. Exalt Him and His name. Take a few minutes to reflect on these verses and do this out loud now.

Notice the use of plural pronouns in Matthew 6:9-15. What is the importance of this to your personal time with God? Remember the context of this passage! You are alone with God and no one else is with you! So why doesn't Jesus tell us to address the Father as "my" Father? What is the significance of using the plural here?

Paul puts this principle into action in Ephesians 6:18-20. What does Paul ask the Ephesians to do?

We need to pray for others about the things that God is calling each of us to do. We shouldn't just talk to God about our needs since He already knows those needs (Matthew 6:8). We are to pursue what is on God's Heart and lift up others before God regarding each of the things that are on His Heart! So, what is on His Heart? That is what we will begin to consider this next week. For now, talk to God about what your attitude towards others has been in your prayer life or personal time with God. Have you included others, been concerned about them, asked God to work in their lives, or has it been all about you? Certainly, God wants to meet your personal needs but that is a very basic view of time with Him. We are a family. A family loves each other. Have you shown love to others through your intercessory prayer life in your personal time with God?

What will you do about it?

Talk to God about others that He brings to your mind now. List them by name and what you are praying for them:

DAY NINE – WHAT'S IN A NAME?

*Hallowed be **Thy name**.*
—*Matthew 6:9*

God spoke further to Moses and said to him, 'I am the Lord (Yahweh); and I appeared to Abraham, Isaac, and Jacob, as God Almighty (El Shaddai), but by My name, Lord (Yahweh), I did not make Myself known to them. (Note: the words in parentheses denote the previous word in Hebrew.)
—*Exodus 6:2,3*

And the Lord descended in the cloud and stood there with him (Moses) as he called upon the name of the Lord. Then the Lord passed by in front of him and proclaimed, 'The Lord, the Lord God, compassionate and gracious, slow to anger, and abounding in lovingkindness and truth; who keeps lovingkindness for thousands, who forgives iniquity, transgression and sin; yet He will by no means leave the guilty unpunished, visiting the iniquity of fathers on the children and on the grandchildren to the third and fourth generations.
—*Exodus 34:5-7*

Read through the verses above again but now put the descriptions about God into your own words to lift-up Him and His name. Take a few minutes to do this before you continue here.

Whose 'name' is to be the focus of our prayers?

This may sound like a simple question, but it isn't. Think about this again and why it might be significant.

The focus of this petition is God's name. It isn't your name, someone else's or a saint of old. It is God's name.

95

Why is this so important to note here?

What's in a name? What does a name signify?

Paul van Imschoot in his Theology of the Old Testament makes this comment about His name:

> In the eyes of the ancients the name was not a simple label distinguishing one individual from his kinsmen. It is an integrating part of the person; what has no name is, so to speak, non-existent... Moreover, the name is supposed to correspond to the essence of the object, and consequently reveals it.[18]

Ron Allen then says that, "Meaning, character, essence, and personality are in a name. Now if these observations are true of human names, how much more true must they be of the name of God."[19]

From the above description about the value and worth of a name, what stands out to you?

What does Jesus do with God's name in John 17:6?

---

[18]Ron Allen, *"What's in a name?"* in *God – What is He Like?* compiled by William F. Kerr (Wheaton, IL., Tyndale House Publishers, 1977), 109.

[19]Ibid., 110.

Since the name is the name of God – *everything* is in that name: life, reality, ultimate perfection, and relationship to the living God! His name encompasses all of life and reality.

What is also true about His name from Philippians 2:9?

His name is above all names. Did you notice that this text speaks of Jesus?

In John 14:8 Philip asks Jesus a question regarding the Father. What is it and how does Jesus respond in verse 9?

Jesus is the revealer of the Father. In Him we see what God is like. It is also true that only through Jesus can anyone come to the Father – John 14:6. To not accept Jesus is to not accept the Father. (cf. John 8:19)

When God is called "I AM" in scripture it refers to His proper name "Yahweh." Notice this point from an explanation of Exodus 3:14-15 by Dr. William Kerr:

...we may make an observation concerning the relationship of the two terms, "I AM" (v. 14) and

"Yahweh" (v. 15). While these seem to be remote from each other, they are closely related. Both terms are forms of the Hebrew verb "to be." The English translation of the Hebrew word in verse 14 (*'ehyeh*) as "I AM," reflects the fact that this verb is a first-person form of the root. The word "Yahweh" is merely the transliteration of the third person of the same verb. Hence, Yahweh means "HE IS." Whereas in Exodus 3:14 God says of himself, "I AM," when we speak of him we do not say "I AM," but rather "HE IS." It is for that reason that the third person form of the verb, namely Yahweh, has come down through history as the *Name* of God, as stated clearly in verse 15.[20]

It should not surprise us to find in the New Testament that the verb "to be" is again used as God's name. We see it in John 8:58 where Jesus is called "I AM." And in John 6:20 when Jesus walks on the water the disciples are told to stop fearing. Why? Because of who is there, "I AM." (Note that English translations take this as a statement translating it as 'it is I' but the Greek behind this has an emphatic "I" *(egw)* with the verb "to be" *(eimi)* which emphasizes the truth of the one the disciples are seeing. It is "I AM.")

So, think about that first question again, whose name is the focus of your prayer?

---

[20] William F. Kerr, ed. *God What is He Like?* (Wheaton, IL: Tyndale House Publishers, 1977), 123-124.

What does His name mean?

How do you think of Him when you come into His presence?

What changes do you need to make?

Pray for others who come to mind or are on your prayer list who need to think more clearly about who they are approaching in their time with God.

DAY TEN – BEFORE THE THRONE

...who art in heaven,...
—Matthew 6:9

Therefore let us draw near with confidence to the throne of grace, so that we may receive mercy and find grace to help in time of need.
—Hebrews 4:16

Using the brief references above, tell God how you see Him. Try to tell Him at least two or three things in light of these verses.

What comes to mind when you think of heaven?

Read **one** of the following pictures of the heavenly scene and tell God what comes to your heart as you read it:

Ezekiel's picture in Ezekiel 1:4-28.
Isaiah's picture in Isaiah 6:1-8.
John's picture in Revelation 1:12-18; 4:1-5:14; 19:1-6.

According to Matthew 5:34, what is heaven?

How do you approach a person on a throne?

Does it make a difference in how you approach Him? Consider the advice in these two passages:

Ecclesiastes 5:2 –

Hebrews 4:16 –

When we come before Him we come with an unusual blend of emotions according to Psalm 2:10, what two different emotions are experienced before God?

Do these emotions also show up in our relationship with God in the New Testament? Read I John 1:4, I Peter 1:8; Philippians 2:12, and I Peter 1:17 and then comment on this question.

(Note: In Psalm 2 the rejoicing is the result of the privilege of serving but it should be tempered with a corresponding true knowledge of God that includes trembling. For a believer under the new covenant there is still rejoicing because we are one of His children and trembling because He is God.)

How do you approach God now?

Are any changes needed?

Remember: You are being brought into the very throne room of God in heaven when you meet with Him! Pray for others who need to realize who they are coming before and that they are being brought into the very throne room of God in heaven.

DAY ELEVEN - HONOR HIS NAME

Hallowed be *Thy name.*
—*Matthew 6:9*

On earth *as it is in heaven.*
—*Matthew 6:10*

O Lord, there is none like Thee, neither is there any God besides Thee, according to all that we have heard with our ears. ... And let Thy name be established and magnified forever.
—*I Chronicles 17:20, 24*

There is no one holy like the Lord, indeed, there is no one besides Thee, nor is there any rock like our God.
—*I Samuel 2:2*

Read Isaiah 6:1-5.

The term "hallowed" means 'separate,' 'other,' 'lifted up,' 'honored,' 'holy.' It is not a part of the address "Our Father," but the first petition. It is a request that God's name be honored here on earth as it is in heaven. We are to ask this privately in our personal time with God. But there is more to this request. It is not acquiescing, personally retreating or giving in to God being God although submission to Him is involved. It is an active response, a wholehearted embracing of God, a coming to His point of view and wanting it more than anything else. There is energy behind this request. It is reverently calling upon God to lift up, honor, and exalt His name on earth as it is in heaven. From the context of the lesson on prayer this begins within our own private time with God as we personally do this in what we say to God. Notice how this is done in the prayers in the Scriptures above. Sometimes it is a call for God to lift

103

up or honor His name and other times the words themselves are expressions of actually doing this. We tell God how great He is, we lift Him up and honor His name by our descriptions of Him. This is the Adoration aspect of prayer in the A.C.T.S. acrostic. And yet it is much more. It is us in God's presence before His throne in heaven as His own child calling upon Him to do what is on His Heart – magnify His Name.

Look back at the verses listed at the start of this day's devotional and re-read Isaiah 6:1-5. Using these verses tell God who He is and what He has done and is doing. Exalt His name using the very words in these verses to inform and guide your worship. Take a few minutes to do this then think about the questions below.

Has this practice been reflected in your personal time with God?

What adjustments do you think you need to make to how you start your time with God in light of this?

How would knowing more about God's nature, attributes, character, and actions from His Word improve this part of your time with God?

Take a minute to evaluate your heart: Do you really want His name to be set apart, treated as holy other, honored, lifted up, exalted, here on earth as it is in heaven? Why or why not?

Honoring God's name needs to begin with our words, in our personal time with God, in our private closet, when it is only the two of us before it can affect our public words and actions.

Who could you tell your plans to in this area who would be willing to ask you if you are doing them?

When will you ask him or her?

What will you ask him or her to hold you accountable to? Be specific and make it "time-bound" so it is measurable.

Pray for others who you know that need to embrace the honoring of His name in their lives. (List them below.)

DAY TWELVE – HONOR HIM

Hallowed be Thy name. ...On earth as it is in heaven.
—Matthew 6:9-10

So then, my beloved, just as you have always obeyed, not as in my presence only, but now much more in my absence, work out your salvation with fear and trembling; for it is God who is at work in you, both to will and to work for His good pleasure. Do all things without grumbling or disputing; that you may prove yourselves to be blameless and innocent, children of God above reproach in the midst of a crooked and perverse generation, among whom you appear as lights in the world, holding fast the word of life, so that in the day of Christ I may have cause to glory because I did not run in vain nor toil in vain.
—Philippians 2:12-16

If we really want His name to be "hallowed," "treated as holy," "lifted up," "be transcendent in our thoughts and life," and "held as awesome in majesty here and now" then we need to allow God to not only produce this desire in us but work it out in our daily actions. Tell God how you want His name to be viewed like here in this world today. Use the above verses to direct your thoughts. After a few moments, turn your focus to His Word and the questions below.

What does Philippians 2:12-16 say this will look like in terms of how we live our lives?

What does this say about being real with God about our feelings, thoughts and attitude towards Him?

How could practicing this passage help us live more like we have a true understanding of God and who He is?

Think about this:

> *No attribute of God is more dreadful to sinners than His holiness.* —Matthew Henry

> *We have learned to live with unholiness and have come to look upon it as the natural and expected thing.* —A.W. Tozer

Do you think our culture has lulled or rocked us asleep to God's true character and nature? Why or why not?

How do you keep a real sense of who He is before you day to day based upon the Philippians passage?

What could you do to keep God in focus as He really is in your mind and heart every day?

Moses' uses the terms "holy" and "honored" in parallel in Leviticus 10:3,

> Then Moses said to Aaron, "It is what the
> Lord spoke, saying,
> 'By those who come near Me I will be treated as
> holy.
> And before all the people I will be honored.'"
> So Aaron, therefore, kept silent.

Read Leviticus 10:1-3 and note what had happened. Why does Aaron refrain from speaking here?

If you have ever lost a loved one you understand the emotions moving through Aaron's heart. What can be learned here about treating God as "holy" and "honored" before God's people?

Pray for those who you know who need to live out in their daily lives what they believe about God, treating Him as holy other, awesomely different, and separate from us. Who are you praying for today? List them here:

DAY THIRTEEN – A STEP OF FAITH: TRUST

Those who know your name put their trust in you.
                                    —Psalm 9:10

Hallowed be Thy name...Give us this day our daily bread.
                                    —Matthew 6:9b, 11

Read Psalm 3.

How does David begin this prayer?

What does He immediately move to in verses 3-6?

Why is it important to do this?

Take a moment to make the thoughts of verses 3-6 about God your thoughts and tell God how you see Him.

According to Psalm 9:10, where should you place your trust?

In this passage, what is it that moves a person to trust God?

Notice that those who know God's name – know who He is and what He does – are moved to trust Him.

Someone has wisely said, "Trust is best developed in the context of a loving family." What do you think? Do you agree or disagree? Why?

How does this relate to being in God's family?

Based upon the following passages, what is the value of trusting in God?

Psalm 37:3-6 –

Psalm 56:11 –

Matthew 6:8 and 26–

Since trusting God is directly related to how well we know the object of our faith (confidence or trust), what will you do to get to know Him better?

Pray for those who need to learn what you discovered today from your time with Him.

DAY FOURTEEN – DAILY FOOD

My food is to do the will of Him who sent Me, and to accomplish His work.
—*John 4:34*

I have treasured the words of His mouth more than my necessary food.
—*Job 23:12*

Give us this day our daily bread.
—*Matthew 6:11*

Read Matthew 6:19-34. Tell Him who He is based upon this passage.

Now think about these questions:

What should your heart be set upon?

How is a believer's lifestyle and a non-believer's lifestyle contrasted?

When you place your trust in God what does He take care of in terms of your "real" needs? (See Matthew 6:33)

How far into the future should you be concerned about? (Matthew 6:11, 34)

113

Does that mean we aren't to do long range planning? Why or why not?

Read James 4:13-15 to check your answer to the above question. How does this passage affect what you said above?

What does focusing upon one day at a time do?

How much faith does it take to see God meet your basic needs? (Read Matthew 6:30)

Would seeing more clearly who God is and what He is like make a difference in your ability to trust Him for your personal needs or even daily food? Why or why not? (Remember those who heard this message lived day to day for their food.)

Take time to thank God for taking care of your needs. Pray for those you know who have unmet physical needs right now. Pray they will see more clearly what God is like and who He really is as a Father to them. Be specific:

DAY FIFTEEN – A DAILY TIME

Give us this day our daily bread.
—Matthew 6:11

But an hour is coming, and now is, when the true worshipers
will worship the Father in spirit and truth; for such people
the Father seeks to be His worshipers.
—John 4:23

In the morning, O Lord, Thou wilt hear my voice; In the
morning, I will order my prayer to Thee and eagerly watch.
—Psalm 5:3

Read John 15:14 and Exodus 33:11. Talk to God today as though He is your best friend and He wants to spend time with you. Tell Him of your desire to meet with Him. Tell Him who He is to you.

Now, read the following passages and think about how often and when we should meet with God: (Note we are working on understanding the phrase in Matthew 6:11.)

Job 1:5 –

Psalm 55:17 –

Daniel 6:10 –

Matthew 6:11 –

There are several things you should have noted from these passages. First, our time with God should be daily (Matthew 6:11). Second, there is a higher principle in practice here that you may not have noticed. It is found in Matthew 6:11 and in John 4:31-34.

What do you think it is?

Now read Job 23:12. What is most important to Job?

The principle is that the spiritual takes priority over the physical.

This is a simple principle that was set up by God when He instituted the temple services in Jerusalem. There was to be a morning and an evening sacrifice. People would come to the temple at both times for prayer and then go home for a mid-day meal and then their evening meal.

For the common person, it was also true that they usually only had two meals a day and so meeting with God twice daily before eating made sense in light of this basic principle.

But what are we to say about David and Daniel? They both spent three times a day with God! They were both extremely busy men high up in authority where they served. Why would they have done something different than the common person who spent two times a day at the temple? As it turns out, it was typical for those who had more financial means to start the day with a 'breakfast' of sorts with nuts, grains, and some fruit. Considering this, you will find these men rising before dawn to meet with God first and then eating a breakfast. It appears that what was most important was putting one's spiritual needs above one's own physical needs.

Do you see this principle practiced with Peter in Acts 10:9-16?

If God is trying to get you to meet with Him daily and before eating, what changes do you need to make to align yourself with when He is trying to get you to meet with Him?

Ask God to teach you more on this. Realize that the people who had three daily meetings with God were all older in their faith! However, both Jonathan Edwards and John Wesley spent three times a day with God from their youth. Don't get overly zealous about what you need to do and find yourself acting out of duty. However, we do need to progress in the faith and not plateau in it. In the same way, our devotional life should not plateau and certainly not digress but move forward just like our sanctification moves progressively towards greater Christlikeness.

Remember, we will not "arrive" in any aspect of our spiritual growth here on earth. Growth is the goal; it is progressive. Therefore, what is the next step you need to take to progress in maturing your devotional life in terms of "when" you meet with God?

How would you evaluate I Thessalonians 5:17 in light of this?

117

Praying is as much an attitude as a time. Taking specific times with God is expected daily. However, talking to Him and aligning ourselves with Him and His will is to be a continual moment by moment, decision by decision, practice – this is praying at all times.

Begin praying that you will be sensitive to God's leading from His Word as to when you will meet with Him. Also, pray for others you know who need to begin hearing what God is saying about when and how often He is moving in their hearts for them to meet with Him.

DAY SIXTEEN – PROPER FOCUS

*But seek first His kingdom and His righteousness; and all
these things shall be added to you.*
—Matthew 6:33

*Whom have I in heaven but Thee? And besides Thee, I desire
nothing on earth.*
—Psalm 73:25

Read and use Psalm 93 to express your thoughts about
God back to Him in worship. Use short sentences. Write
down a few that caught your attention:

From Matthew 6:33, is there a difference between
focusing upon your needs versus God's kingdom? What
is it?

Read Matthew 13:22, what happened to these people?
Why?

What do you tend to focus upon?

What should you do now?

Pray for those who are so entangled with meeting life's basic needs that they never re-focus their thoughts on God and what He is doing. Again, be specific:

DAY SEVENTEEN – THE KINGDOM

***Thy kingdom** come.*

—*Matthew 6:10*

There are three essential elements to a kingdom:

A ruler with adequate authority and power; a realm of subjects to be ruled; and the actual exercise of the function of rulership.[21]

Begin today by telling God about your desire for His righteous reign, rule, and kingdom to physically come to earth here and now.

After a few minutes look up the listed verses that expand on the Kingdom request here in Matthew 6:10. What do these verses say that the kingdom is like?

I Corinthians 15:20-28 –

Acts 1:6-11 –

Matthew 25:31-46 –

Revelation 20:1-6 –

Revelation 21:1 –

As you consider the coming kingdom that will be physically present on this earth, do you want it to come?

---

[21] McClain, *The Greatness of the Kingdom*, 17.

This request, "Thy kingdom come" comes from God! It expresses the very heart of God. It is what He wants. We are not just requesting this of God, we are being urgent and energetic in calling upon God to do this. It is to be our heart's daily pursuit in our personal time with God first and then it is to be acted upon in the living out of our daily life. If it doesn't start privately with God it will never surface in living it out in our daily life.

Do you want Him to rule in your heart today, now, on this earth?

Do you want Him to rule in other's hearts today, now, on this earth?

Consider these quotes: "To pray, 'Thy kingdom come,' means nothing more or less than, 'Christ reign, here and now.'"[22] "That glorious day is coming, and in the meantime the kingdom is in your midst as He reigns and rules in the hearts of His people."[23]
Pray for those you know who need to embrace His coming kingdom and who need to really want it.

---

[22] MacArthur, *Jesus' Pattern of Prayer*, 52.
[23] Ibid., 62.

DAY EIGHTEEN – THE KING

Heed the sound of my cry for help, my King and my God, for to Thee do I pray.
—Psalm 5:2

The Lord is King forever and ever.
—Psalm 10:16

I am the Lord, your Holy One, the Creator of Israel, your King.
—Isaiah 43:15

For this reason also, God highly exalted Him, and bestowed on Him the name which is above every name, so that at the name of Jesus every knee will bow, of those who are in heaven and on earth and under the earth, and that every tongue will confess that Jesus Christ is Lord, to the glory of God the Father.
—Philippians 2:9-11

What do these verses say about who our King is and what He is like?

I Timothy 6:13-16 –

Revelation 17:14 –

Revelation 19:11-16 –

Take a few moments and express your heart to God considering His Kingship then continue this day's devotional.

God reigns as King. Do you believe it? Do you want it?

What does Romans 14:11 and Philippians 2:9-11 say will happen in the future?

Does Jesus Christ reign in your life as Lord and King now?

If not now when?

Pray for others who need to allow Him to reign today in their lives as Lord and King. Be specific:

Pray also for those who still need to accept Him as Savior and Lord. Be specific:

DAY NINETEEN – KINGDOM KIDS

But you are a chosen race, a royal priesthood, a holy nation,
a people for God's own possession so that you may proclaim
the excellencies of Him who has called you out of darkness
into His marvelous light, you had not received mercy, but
now you have received mercy. Beloved, I urge you as aliens
and strangers.
—*I Peter 2:9-11a*

Therefore you are no longer a slave, but a son; and if a son,
then an heir through God.
—*Galatians 4:7*

So then you are no longer strangers and aliens, but you are
fellow citizens with the saints, and of God's household.
—*Ephesians 2:19*

Read Psalm 97. Make these your thoughts towards God. Honor Him and His name with these truths. Take time to do this now and then continue with what follows below.

What has God done for you according to Colossians 1:13-14?

What are we to be looking forward to?

James 2:5 –

I Peter 2:9-10 –

Revelation 5:9-10 –

Revelation 20:6 –

According to these passages who are we as believers?

Who do we represent?

How should we understand what is being said here?

How do we do this 'on earth as it is in heaven?'

Pray for those who need to see themselves as representing the King. Be specific:

DAY TWENTY – A STEP OF FAITH: CONFESSION

Your Kingdom Come...And forgive us our debts, as we also have forgiven our debtors.
—Matthew 6:10b,12

Read Isaiah 6:1-13.

Express to God what this passage adds to your understanding of what God is like.

When we see God as King what is our proper response?

How did Isaiah respond?

When God cleanses a person from their sin, what are they ready for?

When you consider what His kingdom is like you will find areas of your life that are not measuring up to His perfection. Read the Sermon on the Mount in Matthew 5-7. What does this passage say His kingdom is like and what our response should look like?

Take time to confess to God any area of your life that needs to change. Then read 1 John 1:9.

Pray for others to see themselves in light of what His kingdom looks like and to allow God to move them to take this step of faith by honestly confessing what He reveals.

DAY TWENTY-ONE – EXPERIENCING PERSONAL FORGIVENESS

*And **forgive us our debts,** as we also have forgiven our debtors.*

—Matthew 6:12

Read I John 1:5-10.

What is God like? Tell Him how you see Him because of these verses. Describe to Him the picture you see of Him.

Read Psalm 32:1-5.

How does God deal with our sin?

What do we need to do?

If we don't confess, agree with God concerning our sin, what can it do to our vitality?

Matthew 6:12 says we are to ask God for forgiveness. He knows our psychological needs. We need to have vertical forgiveness with God. We need to have "peace" with God. He makes this possible. Why is this step so important for a believer to experience?

His Heart, My Heart – Devotional Transformation
Read Psalm 139:23-24.

Take a several minutes to allow God to point out to you any area of your life that is not pleasing to Him. Do not rationalize away or ignore what He says to you. Whatever comes to mind is what you must deal with before Him.

After a few minutes, thank God for forgiving you and cleansing you from all filthiness and uncleanness.

Pray for others who need to experience God's love and forgiveness today. Be specific:

DAY TWENTY-TWO – FAMILY FORGIVENESS

And forgive us our debts, ***as we also have forgiven our debtors.***

—*Matthew 6:12*

Read Psalm 86:1-10.

Reflect on God's provision for your needs. Tell Him how you see Him because of this passage.

Read James 5:16.

Should the family of believers be a "safe place" to share our faults? Why?

Why are we reluctant to share our faults?

How could it become a "safe place" to share?

How are we to respond to others?

2 Corinthians 2:5-9 –

Ephesians 4:32 –

Colossians 3:12-14 –

What is the basis for our forgiving of others?

If we forgave others the same way Jesus forgives us we would choose not to bring a confessed fault back into our relationship with anyone. It doesn't mean we will forget. It means we do the hard work of putting it under the cross every time it comes back to mind. We choose not to let it control our thoughts or actions. We choose to treat it as forgiven and under the cross. The more we do this the more it will become a habit and eventually we will do it without having to think about it!

Should we take the initiative to restore fellowship with other believers?

Matthew 18:15-17 –

Matthew 5:23,24 –

Galatians 6:1,2 –

Applications to consider:

Is there someone you need to forgive?

Do you need to go to them personally?

When will you do this?

133

Pray for others who need to learn to forgive other believers and live in harmony with one another.

DAY TWENTY-THREE – EXTENDING FORGIVENESS

For if you forgive men for their transgressions, your heavenly Father will also forgive you. But if you do not forgive men, then your Father will not forgive your transgressions.
—Matthew 6:14, 15

In Him we have redemption through His blood, the forgiveness of our trespasses, according to the riches of His grace, which He lavished upon us.
—Ephesians 1:7,8a

Read the verses above and use them to tell God how we are to view Him.

Read Matthew 9:9-13 and John 4:34-42. Did Jesus extend forgiveness to others? How?

What is the extent of His sacrifice upon the cross?

I John 2:1-2 –

John 3:16 –

Read Ephesians 2:1-10.

Why do others need forgiveness?

How should we be involved in offering it to others?

When you forgive another person, do it unconditionally. Remember that you have done more to offend God than any other person could ever do to offend you.

Pray for others who have yet to experience God's love and forgiveness. Pray for divine opportunities to tell them of His love and be prepared to share the good news with them. Write down any names that come to mind here:

DAY TWENTY-FOUR – KNOWING GOD'S WILL

Thy will be done, *on earth as it is in heaven.*
—Matthew 6:10b

Read Psalm 40:8.
How should we respond to God's will?

Do you want it? Why?

In Matthew 6:10, it indicates that we are to call upon God to do His will. When we do this, we are aligning our hearts with what is on God's heart, embracing it, desperately desiring it, with our whole heart, mind, and strength. Can you say honestly that you have this heart response to God's will? Why or why not?

This is to be a daily practice. How are you doing with this?

Take a few moments and tell God how you value Him and His will. Exalt Him and what He wants with your words to Him.

Now read Ephesians 5:15-17.

Where do we find God's will?

Why is it important? (cf. 2 Timothy 3:16-17)

Read John 4:34.
Do you desire to do His will more than your daily
food?

How are you doing on discovering His will from His
Word?

God's will is not a mystery. He has revealed it clearly
in His Word. Knowing God's will and doing it is a matter
of being rightly related to the work of the Holy Spirit in
our lives on a moment by moment basis. If we are
delighting ourselves in God then what He wants will be
the desire of our heart. This is the sense of Psalm 37:4
which says, "Delight yourself in the Lord; And He will
give you the desires of your heart." Or as Augustine said,
"Love God and do what you want." God never leads
contrary to His Word and He always leads in alignment
with His Word. So, the only question is, "Are you in His
Word?"

Are you developing head knowledge and heart knowledge as you spend time in His Word? How?

In other words, are you asking, "Lord what does this mean for me, today, now, in my life?" If it is just information and doesn't move the eighteen inches from your head to your heart it isn't moving into relational knowledge of God that moves you towards reflecting Him.

Are you responding by wanting it urgently, desperately, and asking God to do it?

Pray for those who need to learn God's will. Pray Ephesians 3:14-19 for them. List who you are praying this prayer for here:

DAY TWENTY-FIVE – DOING GOD'S WILL

Your will be done...And do not lead us into temptation, but deliver us from evil.
—Matthew 6:10b, 13a

But prove yourselves doers of the word, and not merely hearers who delude themselves.
—James 1:22

Turn to Appendix 1 in the back of this book. Read through the different names of God and what they mean. Pick out two or three that catch your attention and use them to tell God who He is and what He does.

Read Psalm 1 and describe below the value of delighting yourself in God's Word:

Read Romans 12:1-2.
What should we actively do?

What is to be our goal?

How strongly do you want this?

Are you in alignment with what is on God's heart or do you need to ask God to help you with your "want to?"

If you ask God to move you to "want what He wants" how can you know that He will do what you asked? (See Philippians 2:13)

Trust God and His Word by faith – have trust/confidence in Him and what He says.

141

Apart from God, do you have the power to do His will? Why or why not? (Check out Romans 7:14-25)

Where does the power come from? (Read Romans 8:1-11)

Since you have God dwelling in you as a believer, you have a new nature, His very presence residing within you. You have the resources to do God's will as found in His Word.

Pray for those who know God's will, His Word, but are not doing it.

DAY TWENTY-SIX – A STEP OF FAITH: DEPENDENCE

Your will be done...And do not lead us into temptation, but deliver us from evil.
—Matthew 6:10b, 13a

So then do not be foolish, but understand what the will of the Lord is. And do not get drunk with wine, for that is dissipation, but be filled with the Spirit, speaking to one another in psalms and hymns and spiritual songs, singing and making melody with your heart to the Lord; always giving thanks for all things in the name of our Lord Jesus Christ to God, even the Father; and be subject to one another in the fear of Christ.
—Ephesians 5:17-21

Let the word of Christ richly dwell within you, with all wisdom teaching and admonishing one another with psalms and hymns and spiritual songs, singing with thankfulness in your hearts to God. And whatever you do in word or deed, do all in the name of the Lord Jesus, giving thanks through Him to God the Father.
—Colossians 3:16-17

Turn again to Appendix 1 and pick out two to three different names of God and use them to exalt His name in worship. Tell Him who he is and what He does.

Now read through the above verses in italics and describe what you see:

God enables you by His Spirit to live out what He prescribes in His Word. How does He do this?

143

In the above passages, what is the relationship between being "Word-filled" and "Spirit-filled?"

When we are being led by the Spirit (Romans 8:14), walking in the power of the Holy Spirit (Galatians 5:16), living by the Spirit (Galatians 5:25) we are able to do His will. Therefore, knowing God's will plus stepping out in dependence (faith) upon the Holy Spirit (Philippians 2:13) will result in real life transformation. The evidence of this will be seen in both general results and a specific result when we act upon God's word by faith in the power of the Holy Spirit.

What are the general results of doing God's will (His word) in His strength according to Ephesians 5:19-21?

Have you ever seen any of these general evidences of spiritual life in your own life or in any other believers? If so, when?

What is the specific result of being 'Word-filled' or 'Spirit-filled?' (See Ephesians 5:17)

Since we are to "understand what the will of the Lord is" and "be filled with the Spirit" then the specific result would be simply experiencing the ability to do His will (His word) in His power. Understanding what God's word says and knowing how to apply it to a specific real-life opportunity is what it means to be wise. Doing it in God's power (Ephesians 5:18) is a step of faith in dependence upon Him to do it in that situation through you.

As we walk with God there will be times when we discover His will and depend upon His power to act wisely and do it in a specific opportunity. But there will also be times when we discover His will and fail to act wisely according to His Word. When this happens, we must confess it. As soon as we confess our failure we should be able to turn around and immediately act by faith to do His will instead of sinning. In other words, after we confess, we should be able in His power to do what we just confessed that we failed to do in our own power!

Take time to ask God to show you any area of your life that is displeasing to Him or where you have failed to act wisely in doing His will (His word) in a specific opportunity and confess that to Him. Remember: whatever just popped into your mind is exactly what God wants you to confess – don't argue or rationalize it away – you will never win an argument with God!

Now by faith take a step of faith and depend upon Him to do what you just failed to do.

Pray for others who need to take steps of faith in dependence upon God's Spirit in their lives to do God's word (will). Pray each believer will allow the Holy Spirit to not just be resident but also president in his or her life for God!

DAY TWENTY-SEVEN – TEMPTATION

*And do not lead us into **temptation**.*
—Matthew 6:13

No temptation has overtaken you but such as is common to man; and God is faithful, who will not allow you to be tempted beyond what you are able, but with the temptation will provide the way of escape also, that you may be able to endure it.
—Corinthians 10:13

Turn to Appendix #1 and focus in on these names of God ('El, 'El Shaddai, and Yahweh Tsebhaoth) and exalt God using the truths found there about Him.

Read Psalm 51.
What did David struggle with?

Compare this confession with 2 Samuel 11-12.

According to James 1:13-15, where does temptation come from?

Temptation can be intensified by the Devil but it doesn't come from him. Instead, it comes from the abuse of your desires. It comes from within you – from the corruption that still resides within you from the sin nature.

How can the world influence us based upon I John 2:15-17?

What should we note about the world and all it offers?

During the thousand-year reign of Christ (Revelation 20) our enemy – the Devil – will be bound along with his fallen cohorts and still sin will reign and death will take place according to Isaiah 65:20. In light of this, what will this time of history show us about the sin nature resident in human flesh? (cf. Isaiah 65:20)

Based upon Galatians 5:16-25 we can be victorious over its effects upon us. How is this done?

How are the following passages important in dealing with the corruption still resident within us from the sin nature and the temptation it causes?

I John 1:5-7 –

Romans 8:1-11 –

Philippians 4:8 –

Realize that temptation is not sin. Having an evil thought that passes through your mind is not sin but choosing to do it would be sin. We are tempted when we get "carried away" from moving in the correct, godly, righteous, path for God's glory and are "enticed" by another path that isn't God's by evaluating it and considering its worth but in all this we have not yet sinned. Even though we get distracted from our current path we haven't left it. Even though we start to consider the worth and value of the alternate path we haven't left the current path – following God and His righteous ways. But according to James 1:13-15 we have left God's righteous path for the new fake path when we make the choice, internally, to do it even before we act upon it. Now it is sin and now we have begun down the wrong, unrighteous, fake path and we will experience negative consequences for this.

149

Pray for those who need victory over temptation and the deeds of the flesh. Pray for those caught in sin and consider how you may be called to help according to Galatians 6:1-2. Be Specific:

DAY TWENTY-EIGHT – OVERCOMING THE EVIL ONE

...but deliver us from evil (the evil one).
—Matthew 6:13

Great and marvelous are Your works, O Lord God, the Almighty; Righteous and true are Your ways, King of the nations! Who will not fear, O Lord, and glorify Your name? For You alone are holy; For all the nations will come and worship before You, For Your righteous acts have been revealed.
—Revelation 15:3b-5

Now the salvation, and the power, and the kingdom of our God and the authority of His Christ have come, for the accuser of our brethren has been thrown down, he who accuses them before our God day and night.
—Revelation 12:10b

You are from God, little children, and have overcome them; because greater is He who is in you than he who is in the world.
—I John 4:4

I do not ask You to take them out of the world, but to keep them from the evil one.
—John 17:15

There is no doubt that all believers face a formidable foe in the evil one – the Devil. However, as you read the verses above what can you be confident about as you face this battle?

Using the above verses about God tell God how great and mighty He is and lift up Him and what he does especially in light of His supremacy and authority over the evil one who is only a created being and not the everlasting, eternal, God. List how you see Him here:

Read Psalm 54.

Are there any thoughts in this passage that are true of your experience? Which ones?

Tell God of your dependence upon Him for victory over the evil one.

What do these passages say about our battle and how to be victorious?

I Peter 5:8-11 –

Ephesians 6:10-20 –

James 4:4-10 –

I John 4:4 –

Confess any failure God reveals in your life as you reflect on these passages and choose to act in faith, depending upon Him, overcoming the enemy and living out the faith in this world!

Where is our victory according to these verses?

I John 5:4 –

I Peter 5:8-9 –

Pray for others who have fallen prey to the enemy. Consider your part in helping them overcome the evil one's influence in their lives. Pray specifically:

DAY TWENTY-NINE – INTERCESSORY PRAYER

I do not ask Thee to take them out of the world, but to keep them from the evil one. They are not of the world, even as I am not of the world. Sanctify them in the truth; Thy word is truth. As Thou didst send Me into the world, I also have sent them into the world.

—John 17:15-18

Our *Father...Give* **us**...**our** *daily...Forgive* **us our**...*as* **we** *forgive*...**our debtors**...*lead* **us**...*deliver* **us**...

—Matthew 6:9-13

Use Jesus' prayer in John 17:15-18 as a basis for talking to God about how you see Him and expressing your acceptance of how He is using you in this world. Take a few moments, read this passage, and lift up the name of God.

Now reflect upon the use of the plurals in the Matthew 6:9-13 passage. What is the point here since this is all done privately, in our own personal time with God, and not publicly based upon the context of this passage? Why is this prayer using plurals – Our Father, give us, forgive us, deliver us?

Read Ephesians 6:18-20.

What should be our attitude in prayer?

Who should we be praying for in light of Paul's comments here?

What specifically does Paul want prayer for here?

Begin a list of others who you need to be constantly praying for in light of what you have discovered today. Remember to pray for those who need provisions, forgiveness, and deliverance. Pray daily for them.

DAY THIRTY – A LIFE OF FAITH

For Yours is the kingdom and the power and the glory forever, Amen.
—*Matthew 6:13b*

And without faith it is impossible to please Him, for he who comes to God must believe that He is and that He is a rewarder of those who seek Him.
—*Hebrews 11:6*

For whatever is born of God overcomes the world; and this is the victory that has overcome the world – our faith.
—*I John 5:4*

Turn to Psalm 104 and express the thoughts in these verses back to God as your own. Exalt His name as you do this. Write down any thoughts that stand out to you:

Read Hebrews 12:1-29.

Why should we seek to be faithful in our walk with God? (Note verse 1)

How should do this? (See Hebrews 12:2-29)

Read Hebrews 11:1-6.
What role does faith play in our lives?

Read Galatians 2:20.
Does this describe your life today? Why or why not?

What needs to happen to reach this lifestyle?

Remember that faith is trust or confidence in the object of our faith. Faith grows stronger as we are in God's Word (Romans 10:17). Little faith doubts and gets overcome by distractions and life's challenges like Peter when he walked on the water towards Jesus (Matthew 14:22-33). He walks all the way to Jesus and only at the end does he take his eyes off of Jesus and gets overcome by the wind and begins to sink. Jesus only has to reach out his arm to rescue him but then says, "You of little faith, why did you doubt?" Note that the strength of our faith is based upon how well we know the object of our faith and keep our thoughts focused on Him. Don't let "possibilities" or "distractions" or "challenges" occupy your thoughts. Take every thought captive to the obedience of Christ (2 Corinthians 10:5). Keep your mind on those things that are true, honorable, right, pure, lovely, of good repute, excellent, and worthy of praise (Philippians 4:8). And note that in verses 6 and 7 of Philippians that if you have any anxious thoughts you should give them to God. He will then guard your hearts and minds with His peace. It is after this that Paul writes verse 8. If you don't refocus your thoughts on what is true, right, etc., then your anxious thoughts can return and you will have to go through this process again to get peace in your heart and mind. It is as Proverbs 23:7a says, "As a man thinks, so is he." What you think about will surface in your actions. The spiritual transformation process is a battle for the mind (Romans 12:2). You must exercise self-control (Galatians 5:23; 2 Peter 1:6) once in the area you are facing and then keep doing it (persevering – cf. 2 Peter 1:6) until it becomes a habit (godliness – cf. 2 Peter 1:7) and you no longer have to think about it as you now supernaturally do it without thinking it through each time.

Pray for others who need to learn to live by faith. Be specific:

DAY THIRTY-ONE – HEAVENLY MINDED

See how great a love the Father has bestowed upon us, that we should be called children of God; and such we are. For this reason the world does not know us, because it did not know Him. Beloved, now we are children of God, and it has not appeared as yet what we shall be. We know that, when He appears, we shall see Him just as He is. And everyone who has this hope fixed on Him purifies himself, just as He is pure.

—I John 3:1-3

Use the verses above to exalt God's name. Think about each thing you say to God as you do this. See some ideas in the light grey comments here:

Lord You are our Loving Father.
You are holy and pure.
You are our sanctification.

Read Psalm 15.

Express in your own words back to God the type of person God is looking for. Write down some of the things God is looking for:

From I John 3:1-3, what is the value of focusing upon heaven to our lives today?

His Heart, My Heart – Devotional Transformation

Read 2 Peter 3:14-18.

In verse 14 Peter says these believers are longing for God's new righteous world where He reigns (note 2 Peter 3:13). In fact, this is the motivation for believers to live now for Him and to do His will. Do you long for the new righteous world where Christ physically reigns here on earth? Why or why not?

What could you do to be more heavenly-minded?

It has been said that some people are so heavenly-minded that they are of no earthly good. However, here in I John 3:1-3 and in 2 Peter 3:14-18 it is exactly the opposite. It is only those who are heavenly-minded that are truly of any earthly good.

Pray for others who need to have a heavenly mindset. (List their names below.)

DAY THIRTY-TWO – FOR HIS GLORY

For Thine is the kingdom, and the power, and the glory,
forever. Amen.
—Matthew 6:13b

This morning reflect on God's glory. Tell Him how you see Him. (Use Ezekiel 1 or Revelation 4 to direct your words to Him.) Write down any thoughts about God that catch your attention:

Express to God your desire to glorify Him (Read John 17 to see how Jesus sought to do this.) What caught your attention from John 17 about Jesus' relationship with His Father?

163

Pray for others to make glorifying God their daily pursuit. Be specific:

DAY THIRTY-THREE – DEVOTIONAL DEVELOPMENT #1

During the last month, you have explored in depth each phrase and term from only one passage – Matthew 6:5-13. Each phrase or term has been explained using a number of parallel passages and cross references. Before launching you into selecting your own passages of Scripture to study in your personal time with God I want to introduce you to how you can move through a Bible book paragraph by paragraph or chapter by chapter. Let's begin with the book of Ephesians. This is where I would make use of a journal and write on one side of the page the passage and on the other side today's date.

Passage: Ephesians 1:1-2   Date: _____

First ask God to speak to you and then read the passage for today. Ask yourself questions about what you read: Who? What? When? Where? Why? and How? Every literary genre has a structure that determines the context from which the words of the text get their meaning. This is how you begin to see what the author of the book intended to communicate.

New Testament Epistles typically begin with an introduction that identifies who wrote it and who it is written to as well as the attitude the author is taking towards them. It also often lays out the overall ideas the author intends to expound upon. Therefore, what can you discover about the author, the readers, and the author's direction in thought for this book from Ephesians 1:1-2?

165

As you read the text look for what the author is talking about and what he is saying about it. This is called the Author's Big Idea. The Author's Big Idea is a complete sentence that interprets the text in "there and then" terms. In other words, it is what the original audience would have understood the author to be saying to them at that time, place, cultural setting, and historical setting. We cannot apply a misunderstood text. And we cannot know what it means to us unless we know what it meant to the original audience. This is the first step in handling the Word of God as a skilled exegete.

Even though these first two verses are the beginning of the letter the author has a "big idea" that can be found here. It is, "God's messenger, Paul, writes to the faithful believers at Ephesus with a message of grace and peace from God." The "Author's Big Idea" here addresses the question, "What is God's message, through Paul, to faithful believers in Ephesus?" The answer is, "Grace and peace from God the Father and the Lord Jesus Christ."

Why would this greeting be important to this audience?

What can you discover about God from these two verses?

What can you discover about the readers of this message?

What can you discover about Paul and his role as a "faithful" messenger?

Although brief, what can the reader expect Paul to say in the rest of the letter based upon this introduction?

Take time to tell God who He is in light of what you just discovered. This is the Honoring His name part of prayer. Maybe you want to say, "God you care about your own. You seek to communicate with them. You have more to say to faithful believers. You continue to invest in their lives." Think about this and tell God how you see Him.

Maybe as you prayed you thought about the term "faithful" as one of the characteristics of those whom God sends His message of grace and peace. Think for a moment about this.

What does this say about Paul?

What does it say about the readers?

Certainly, Paul fits this role as one who is faithful. And the believers here in Ephesus fit this description too. Obviously, as believers today we all want to receive grace from God and be at peace with Him as that is the nature of being in His Kingdom. But are you in that state of existence with Him today, right now?

Are you being "faithful" as a believer? Why or why not?

Do you have a growing confidence that you are a "believer" a "disciple" of the living God?

If you can't answer this in the positive you need to examine yourself. All the book of I John was written so you might "know that you have eternal life" – I John 5:13. If you answered "no" or you were "uncertain" then find time today to read this book and note all the things it says will be true about believers. There are vital signs of spiritual life identified in this book. Is there evidence in your life that you do in fact have life in Him?

Take time to deal with His reign and rule in your life in light of being faithful to Him. Again, you will want to confess any area that comes to mind and then appropriate the power of the Holy Spirit to be faithful. Remember there is nothing natural about what God asks from us it is all supernatural and we need supernatural resources to do what He asks of us.

Now, Seek His Will on earth as it is in heaven. Be faithful in His power to do it. What is He saying to you at this moment that you should be doing? What is He telling you to apply from the passage you looked at today? Write down anything that comes to mind here:

Pray for others who need what you just discovered. List those you are praying for here:

Trust God to make you "faithful" today!

DAY THIRTY-FOUR – DEVOTIONAL DEVELOPMENT #2

Turn to Ephesians 1:3-14 and read it.
What is the "Author's Big Idea" in this text?

(Note: this is a difficult text to quickly find the big idea. Many times, you will find that with just a little study the "Author's Big Idea" becomes clear but in this text, it will take much more time to discover. Realize that in the Greek this passage is all one sentence but in your English text it is several sentences.)

The "Author's Big Idea" of this passage is, "Blessed be God the Father who has blessed believers with every spiritual blessing in the heavens through the Father's selection, the Son's sacrifice, and the Spirit's sealing."

(Notice that the "Author's Big Idea" in "there and then" terms is also the same as the "Big Idea Today" in "here and now" terms. This is because the same truths that applied to the original audience equally apply to believers today. By simply using the term "believers" in the big idea rather than "first century believers in Ephesus" which would have made it just the "Author's Big Idea" the big idea applies to both "then and there" as well as "here and now". However, realize that

171

not every "Author's Big Idea" can be so easily moved into our time – "here and now." Before doing this, you must consider the "degree of transfer" that is possible from the original setting to our setting. It is often immediate. But some "Author Big Ideas" will have to be adjusted to apply to us today. You wouldn't want to think that a call to Noah to build an ark was what you were to do today! But you would want to obey anything that God told you to do. See Appendix III for more information on this skill.)

Reflect on the text of Ephesians 1:3-14.
How has the Father been involved in providing these spiritual blessings to you – what has He done?

How has the Son been involved – what has He done?

How has the Spirit been involved – what has He done?

What do you have to do, according to verse 13, to get these blessings?

Take time now to tell God who He is, what He has done, and how you feel about it. You might say, "You choose me before I was even born. You brought me to yourself. You are God and you do what you please." Think about it from this passage and talk to Him. Write down any thoughts that are especially meaningful to you:

Think through the importance of hearing the message and responding to it. Think about how the Father's, Son's, and Spirit's role all worked together to secure these heavenly blessings for you.

Are you thankful?

Are you moved, like Paul, to praise God?

Is this something that just makes you want to tell others?

Is there something you found in this passage that brings you to a point of confession?

Is there something in this passage that challenges you to depend upon God's power to do?

173

Take time to think of others you know who need to discover what you have from this passage. Pray for them by name.

Take time to thank God for all He has done for you. Today, will you tell one person what God has done for you and praise His name verbally and publicly?

When will you do it? (Be specific as to day and time.)

Who will you tell?

Who knows this application and will ask you if you did do it?

DAY THIRTY-FIVE
DEVOTIONAL DEVELOPMENT #3

Turn to Ephesians 1:15-23 and read it.

New Testament Epistles sometimes include a prayer before the author begins the body of his letter. This not only tells us about the heart of the author towards his readers but also the heart of God towards them. Paul often intersperses prayers within the body of his letters as he does here in Ephesians.

Today you are viewing a prayer of Paul's for believers who are growing in their faith. These believers are already faithful, blessed with every spiritual blessing in the heavens by God and praise God for it. So, what would you pray for believers at this point in their walk with God? Any ideas?

Look at this passage and see if you can identify the "Author's Big Idea" of the passage. Write it down here: (Try it before you turn the page!)

Remember, it takes time to study the text and accurately identify the "Author's Big Idea" and then consider the "degree of transfer" of the "big idea" to us today. You should always ask the question, "What is the degree of transfer of this 'big idea' to us today?"

How did you do with discovering the Author's Big Idea? Was it difficult? Easy? Or did you give up?

The "Author's Big Idea" of this passage is, "Because Paul has heard of the Ephesian believers' faith and love for fellow believers he prays with thankfulness that God would increase their wisdom and knowledge of Him, that they might know the hope of His calling, that they would know what He inherits because of them, and know His power directed towards them as found in the life of Christ".

As you think about this text and the "Author's Big Idea", "How much of this transfers to us today?" We can't say that Paul is now praying this for us, can we? This was what Paul prayed for the Ephesians. But, I don't know any believer's today in Ephesus and I certainly don't know of their faith or if they are acting in love towards one another. What moved Paul to pray was hearing of these believer's faith and love for all the brethren in Christ. Certainly, all believers should know these truths today but shouldn't we think about whether or not having faith in Jesus Christ and love towards all the saints is foundational (required) or not for praying these requests for someone else? Certainly, being a believer would be required but it may or may not be true that we are demonstrating love towards our fellow believers like these Ephesian believers – think of the Corinthian believers who Paul wrote to earlier. What this means is that this time the "Author's Big Idea" won't immediately transfer into our time and culture without some adjustment. So, an adjusted "Big Idea" might be, "Believers who hear of other believers' faith and love for fellow believers should thankfully pray that God would increase their wisdom and knowledge of Him, that they might know the hope of His calling, what He inherits because of them, and His power directed towards them as found in the life of Christ."

If you plan on teaching this somewhere you will also want to condense the "Big Idea Today" into less words – maybe 12 to 15 if possible. This makes it easier to remember but it takes time to do and much thought too without losing the sense of the passage.

As you reflect on this prayer and what it means tell God how you see Him. Tell Him about His great name, His character, and His wonderful acts. Write down any truths that stand out to you:

Think about the things prayed for in this passage. Which requests would you like to study or think about more deeply?

Which ones do you need to understand more?

What can you discover from this passage about God?

About believers?

About God's power?

177

What do you need in light of this prayer?

Do you have faith?

Do you love others?

Pray for others who need the same thing. Be specific and pray by name.

Who is praying for your spiritual growth like Paul does for the Ephesians?

Do you need a discipler in your life who is doing this?

Who could you ask?

Who are you praying for like this?

Who should you be praying for and taking a more intentional and active interest in discipling like Paul does here with these believers?

How and when will you do something about it?

DAY THIRTY-SIX
DEVOTIONAL DEVELOPMENT #4

Turn to Ephesians 2:1-10 and read it.

Write out the "Author's Big Idea" from this passage: (Again, try it but don't get bogged down with trying to do this and miss spending time with God. Do what you can and then let God speak to you.)

The "Author's Big Idea" from this passage is, "Gentile believers were once dead but are now alive by grace through faith in Christ so He can show them the riches of His grace and will do good works as His workmanship."

How much of the "Author's Big Idea" transfers to us today?

Think through this passage. What questions about the "Big Idea" can you create in order to discover all that is here in this passage that Paul writes to the Ephesian believers?

Here are some questions to consider:

What does it mean that these believers were once "dead"?

Why were they "dead"?

How did they once "walk"?

What did they "follow"?

The text says that these believers were "by nature children of wrath" and that this is also the state of "the rest of mankind." (This also makes the "Author's Big Idea" directly transferable to us today!) Therefore, what hope is there for mankind?

How did God step in and solve man's hopeless situation in verses 4-7?

Believers are "alive," "raised up," and "seated with Him," in the heavenly places. Why does God do this according to verse 7?

How did these individuals become "alive" according to verses 5, 8, and 9?

Who are they now based upon verse 10?

In terms of "Honoring God's Name" what about all of this moves you to tell God how great He is and what He has done?

Take time to tell God how you see Him. Honor His Name by telling Him who He is and what He has done.

Think about these questions in light of who God is: Can God take care of all of your needs?

Are you trusting in Him to do this today?

How are God's Kingdom conditions seen in this passage?

Is there anything you need forgiveness for as a result of considering His Kingdom reign as suggested in this passage?

According to verses 7 and 10 what is God's will for believers?

How are you doing with depending upon God's power to do His will in this passage?

Pray for yourself and for others who need to learn the same thing.

Walk through this whole day with God so that "His Heart is Your Heart."

DAY THIRTY-SEVEN – DEVOTIONAL DEVELOPMENT #5

Turn to Ephesians 2:11-22 and read it.
Write out the "Author's Big Idea" of the passage:

Here is the "Author's Big Idea" of the passage, "Believers are to remember they were once lost but in Christ both Gentiles and Jews are now one new man so that together they are at peace with God, have access to the Father, are members of God's household, and are by the Spirit growing into a dwelling for God corporately and individually."

As you read this passage expand on the key points mentioned in the "Author's Big Idea" and how they are expressed here. Ask questions about the text, search the text for answers, and be careful to see what the text says without reading into it something that the author isn't talking about.

Take time to Honor God's Name in light of your discoveries from the passage.

Consider how His Kingdom and Reign are expressed here and consider if you need forgiveness in any area.

What does this passage suggest that "God's Will" is and how you are to be involved?

Think about how you will depend upon God's power to keep the flesh from destroying what God wants and how the Holy Spirit will keep you from the schemes and traps of the enemy as you pursue what He wants.

Pray for others who need the same things you discovered.

Seek to walk in step with Him today!

DAY THIRTY-EIGHT – DEVOTIONAL LAUNCH #1

Begin today to establish your own personal time with God on a daily basis. Let me suggest that you continue to move through the book of Ephesians and finish this book first. However, if that is not your plan you should start by selecting a passage (a paragraph or chapter; a Psalm; a Proverb; etc.) of Scripture to read.

Record your text here: _____ Today's Date: _____

As you read it think about what the author is saying to his audience (there and then) and what he is saying about what he is talking about (the "Author's Big Idea" of the passage). In order to better understand how to discover the "Author's Big Idea" take some time to read Appendix III.

If you attempted to write the "Author's Big Idea" above consider how much of it transfers to us today.

Write the "Big Idea Today" in "here and now" terms – this is what you will want to apply.

In light of this, what is God saying to you from this text?

Now turn your attention to God. Take time now to gain His heart for the day.

Begin with Honoring His Name,
Deal with His reign and rule in your life, and
Seek His Will on earth as it is in heaven.
Pray for others who need what you discover.
List those you are praying for here:

Constantly walk through the day by faith expecting God to live His life through you and do what you just asked Him to do: Honor His Name – not yours; Establish His Reign and Authority – not yours; and Accomplish His Will – not yours. Decide now to Accept and Embrace His Provisions for you: The daily food He provides; Forgiveness along with extending it to others; Deliverance from the effects of the sin nature still resident in you and the schemes and traps of the evil one. Seek to be a vessel today whose Heart beats with what is on His Heart. Live by faith. Expect Him to live through you. Enjoy today's journey by faith.

DAY THIRTY-NINE – DEVOTIONAL LAUNCH #2

As you read your text for today try to discover the "Author's Big Idea". This works best if your text is at least a paragraph from an Epistle or Psalm, or a whole scene from a Narrative section. It is really important to learn to see the author's intended meaning in its full context. So, if you haven't settled on moving through one Psalm in one sitting, one entire Narrative section, or paragraph by paragraph through a New Testament Epistle, then you really need to revise your plan to do this. This will help you see things in context as God recorded His Word and intended for it to be understood. Write your text for the day below and today's date.

Passage: _____ Today's Date: _____

Follow the same pattern as yesterday. As you read your passage think about what the author is saying and what he is saying about what he is saying – the "Author's Big Idea":

Now consider the degree of transfer of the "Author's Big Idea" to us today. Write out the "Big Idea Today" in "here and now" terms:

Note what God is saying to you from this text:

Now turn your attention to God. Take time now to

His Heart, My Heart – Devotional Transformation
gain His heart for the day.

Begin with Honoring His Name,
Deal with His reign and rule in your life, and
Seek His Will on earth as it is in heaven.
Pray for others who need what you discover.
    List those you are praying for here:

Constantly walk through the day by faith expecting God to live His life through you and do what you just asked Him to do: Honor His Name – not yours; Establish His Reign and Authority – not yours; and Accomplish His Will – not yours. Decide now to Accept and Embrace His Provisions for you: The daily food He provides; Forgiveness along with extending it to others; Deliverance from the effects of the sin nature still resident in you and the schemes and traps of the evil one. Seek to be a vessel today whose Heart beats with what is on His Heart. Live by faith. Expect Him to live through you. Again, enjoy today's journey by faith.

188

DAY FORTY – FINAL DEVOTIONAL LAUNCH

Continue as you did yesterday – you are working on establishing a spiritual habit and repetition is necessary to do this. Note that there is now more blank space for you to write and develop your own way of recording your time with God. Once the devotional ends move to your own blank journal, notebook, or electronic journal and continue to develop your time with God.

Passage: _____ Today's Date: _____

What is the author talking about here?

What is he saying about it?

What is the "Author's Big Idea"?

What is the "Big Idea Today" in here and now terms?

What is God speaking to you about today from this text?

What do you need to talk to God about today?

Take time now to:

Honor His Name,
Deal with His reign and rule in your life, and
Seek His Will on earth as it is in heaven.
Pray for others who need what you discover.
List those you are praying for here:

Constantly walk through the day by faith expecting God to live His life through you and do what you just asked Him to do: Honor His Name – not yours; Establish His Reign and Authority – not yours; and Accomplish His Will – not yours. Decide now to Accept and Embrace His Provisions for you: The daily food He provides; Forgiveness along with extending it to others; Deliverance from the corruption that is still residing in your flesh due to the sin nature and deliverance from the evil one.

Pray for others who need to accept or experience God's provisions, His forgiveness, or His deliverance. List the person and need here:

Thank God for your time. Moment by moment, decision by decision, seek today to be a vessel whose Heart beats with what is on His Heart in your personal convictions, character, and conduct. Trust God to live by faith. Expect Him to live through you. Enjoy today's journey by faith.

EXTRA DAY ONE – START YOUR OWN JOURNAL

You should move on now to using your own blank journal to start writing in or start a notebook for your devotional time. The value of starting your own written record of your time with God will help you see how He is speaking to you in your life, provide a record to review later to thank Him for all He has done, and after a year it will provide a way to look back and see what God was doing in your life as you note any patterns He has or is dealing with in your life and any victories you have had along the way. This will give you confidence in moving forward in your walk with God.

Passage: _____ Today's Date: _____

Follow the same pattern as yesterday. As you read your passage think about what the author is saying and what he is saying about what he is saying – the "Author's Big Idea":

Then think about the degree of transfer to us today. What is the "Big Idea Today"?

Then note what God says to you from this text here:

Now turn your attention to God. Take time now to gain His heart for the day. Begin with:

Honoring His Name,
Deal with His reign and rule in your life, and
Seek His Will on earth as it is in heaven.

Pray for others who need what you discover.
List those you are praying for here:

Constantly walk through the day by faith expecting God to live His life through you and do what you just asked Him to do: Honor His Name – not yours; Establish His Reign and Authority – not yours; and Accomplish His Will – not yours. Decide now to Accept and Embrace His Provisions for you: The daily food He provides; Forgiveness along with extending it to others; Deliverance from the effects of the sin nature and deliverance from the evil one. Seek to be a vessel again today whose Heart beats with what is on His Heart. Live by faith. Expect Him to live through you. Enjoy today's journey by faith.

EXTRA DAY TWO – COMMENCEMENT

You have been launched from your personal training time in the biblical practice of the devotional life. Thanks for taking this journey and don't forget this practice is the launch pad for the Christian life and the discipleship process. This is the foundation for all biblical transformation in your life. You should return to this guide as needed to sharpen and improve your devotional life. But you should also move on to the next book, *A Cry from the Heart – Biblical Transformation.*

Remember that the devotional life is never static nor will it cease to develop and become deeper and more intimate so that you can say when you get to heaven,

> *I am no stranger to this place or to the God I now see with my eyes for I have been here a thousand times before and I am more like Him in my thoughts, feelings, choices, and actions then when I first began.*
>
> —a sermon by John Eliot[24]

Passage: _____ Today's Date: _____

---

[24] Charles E. Hambrick-Stowe, *The Practice of Piety* (Chapel Hill, NC: The University of North Carolina Press, 1982), xvi.

EXTRA DAY THREE – REVIEW and CHALLENGE

If you haven't purchased your own blank journal or don't have a notebook yet, please use this one for today. Also, why not take someone else through this study? Use it as your first discipleship tool with another person. You can use the small group discussions as your one-on-one or small group times as you as a group or with an individual walk through each day's devotional. Consider passing this on to others. See you someday with our Lord in Heaven – Glory!

Passage: _____ Today's Date: _____

What is the author talking about here?

What is he saying about it?

What is the "Author's Big Idea"?

What is the big idea in here and now terms?

What is God speaking to you about today from this text?

What do you need to talk to God about today?

Take time now to:

Honor His Name,
Deal with His reign and rule in your life, and
Seek His Will on earth as it is in heaven.
Pray for others who need what you discover.
List those you are praying for here:

Constantly walk through the day by faith expecting God to live His life through you and do what you just asked Him to do: Honor His Name – not yours; Establish His Reign and Authority – not yours; and Accomplish His Will – not yours. Decide now to Accept and Embrace His Provisions for you: The daily food He provides; Forgiveness along with extending it to others; Deliverance from the sin nature and the evil one.

Pray for others who need to accept or experience God's provisions for them, His forgiveness, or His deliverance. List the person and need here:

Thank God for your time. Moment by moment, decision by decision, seek today to be a vessel whose Heart beats with what is on His Heart in your personal convictions, character, and conduct. Trust God to live by faith. Expect Him to live through you. Enjoy today's journey by faith.

Appendix I
Proper Names of God

Proper Names of God

1. Adonai – "God...the ruler to whom everything is subject." Genesis 20:4; Psalm 38:15; 68:17-32; 86:12; Zechariah 9:4
2. 'El – "God...the Lord, strong and mighty." Genesis 1:1; 31:13; 33:20
3. 'Elohim, 'Eloha – "God...the creator and preserver of all things." Genesis 1:2, 27; Job 3:4; Psalm 18:32
4. 'El 'Elyon – "God...the most high and exalted one." Genesis 14:18-20; Numbers 24:16; Isaiah 14:14
5. 'El Olam – "God...the everlasting God." Genesis 21:33
6. 'El Shaddai – "God...the mighty One, who makes nature subservient to grace, possesses all power in heaven and on earth, and is the source of blessing and comfort." Genesis 17:1; 28:3; 35:11; 43:14; 48:3; 49:25; Exodus 6:3; Numbers 24:4; (N.T. eq. 2 Corinthians 6:18 and Revelation 4:8).
7. Yahweh (Jehovah) – "God...the eternal, absolute, self-existent God whose grace and faithfulness endure forever." Exodus 3:13-15; 15:3; Psalm 83:19; Isaiah 42:8; Hosea 12:6.
   a. "I AM" – N.T. equivalent of Yahweh (Exodus 3:14) in Matthew 14:27 and John 6:20
      1) "I AM the bread of life." John 6:35
      2) "I AM the light of the world." John 8:12
      3) "I AM the door of the sheep." John 10:7
      4) "I AM the good shepherd." John 10:11
      5) "I AM the Son of God." John 10:36
      6) "I AM the resurrection and the life." John 11:25
      7) "I AM the way, the truth, and the life." John 14:6

8) "I AM the true vine." John 15:1
b. Jehovah-jireh –"God...our provider." Genesis 22:14
c. Jehovah-rapha – "God...our healer." Exodus 15:26
d. Jehovah-nissi – "God...our banner of victory." Exodus 17:15
e. Jehovah-m'kaddesh   –   "God...our sanctification." Leviticus 20:7,8
f. Jehovah-shalom – "God...our peace." Judges 6:23,24
g. Jehovah-ra-ah   –   "God...our shepherd." Psalm 23:1
h. Jehovah-tsidkenu   –   "God...our righteousness." Jeremiah 23:6
i. Jehovah-shammah – "God...the everpresent one." Ezekiel 48:35
8. Yah – (abbreviation of Yahweh) – Genesis 1:1; Exodus 15:2; Psalm 68:4; 89:8; 135:1. See Hallelu**jah** = Praise Yah!
9. Yahweh Tsebhaoth – (Jehovah of Hosts; Lord of Hosts) – "God...the King in the fullness of His glory, surrounded by organized hosts of angels, governing the entire universe as the Omnipotent One, and in His temple receiving the honor and adoration of all His creatures." I Samuel 1:3; 4:4; Psalm 69:6; 80:4; 84:1, 8; Isaiah 1:24; Amos 9:5; Haggai 2:7-9.

*Adapted and expanded from Herman Bavinck, *The Doctrine of God* (Edinburgh, Scotland: Banner of Truth, 1978), 101-102.

Appendix II

His Heart, My Heart Devotional Transformation Small Group and One-on-One Discussion Guide

Leading Your Transformational One-on-One or Small Group Times

As you lead this group take some time to pray for each member as you prepare and even as you lead it. Listen for anything God says to you. You need to follow what He says.

Each discussion has information that is only for you. Read the Vision for Leaders, Focus, and Goals section. These sections set the stage for the session. You will get the overall picture as to where you are taking the group and what should take place because of it. Make sure you read through the Approach, Discovery, and Decision sections well before the discussion. This is how you A.D.D. value to your discussion.

Throughout this part of the lesson you will see a

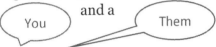 and a

header. You should just read what is under the "You" header and then listen for the responses to your question under the "Them" header. If you don't hear the answer you are expecting you should use an additional question like, "What else do you see?" Your goal is to keep the discussion moving and to not let it lapse into a lecture. Also, never answer your own question – just rephrase it if it wasn't understood. Remember, don't tell them the answer! Don't do it! If they discover it through your questions, there is an 80%-90% chance that they will remember it. This creates greater transformational traction in their lives. Think about this, there is only a 10%-20% chance they will remember it if you tell them. Therefore, ask the questions listed. Now, don't think you must ask these exactly as they are written. You don't! Rephrase them with your own words. But this means you must think through this lesson before coming to lead it.

Also, don't think you must hear every answer that I list under the "Them" section of the guided discussion. Once you have heard one or some you should move to the next question. If you think there is something under the "Them" section that is important and it wasn't shared, and no one says it after you ask them if they have any other responses, then you should just mention it as one of your observations and then ask the next question under the "You" section.

This transformational small group sets the stage for biblical discipleship. After you lead this group you should read my books *A Cry from the Heart – Biblical Transformation* and *Transformed by Truth* and attend the **Transformational Training Seminar**. This will equip you to disciple those in your group from where they are now on through all the stages of discipleship. Check out the books and seminar at: www.hisheartmyheart.org

Enjoy this! Watch how God works through you. Listen to Him. Make the changes He directs you towards as you delight yourself in Him (Psalm 37:4).

His Heart, My Heart
Discussion #1

MY LIFE, HIS LIFE

Vision for Leaders:
  We live at a time when even believers are inventing their own reality of what is true. This is happening in terms of how God is viewed and what it means to be human. However, rather than move from our experience to truth – like is happening in the culture today where what changes is truth and not one's life – we must start with truth and move to experience – if we are really going to see any real-life transformation that is biblical. In Jesus' first sermon out of five in the book of Matthew Jesus sets forth the Kingdom lifestyle for His people. He begins the Sermon on the Mount with both "be" and "do" attitudes and wraps up the sermon with a brief parable. Right in the middle of this entire discourse Jesus places His training on prayer – the devotional life. Therefore, the devotional life becomes central to living the kingdom life.

Focus:
  Only by hearing and following Jesus' words will anyone wisely build his or her life, and endure the challenges, difficulties, and sufferings of life.

Goals:
  To know that what you build your life upon will determine how life's challenges will affect you.
  To feel your need to be in God's Word discovering wisdom for life every day.
  _To do_ **His Heart, My Heart – Devotional Transformation** every day in order to become wise,

moment by moment, spirit-filled image bearers of God as a daily habit.

Approach:

"What does it take to build a stable house?"

Skilled workers, level ground, and a firm foundation.

"When someone mentions the "foundation" ask the group: "Why is the foundation so important?"

It determines the stability of the whole building.

"What needs to be considered when it is built?"

What the ground is like where the building is being built. Is it on rock, dirt, clay, sand, etc.

"Why is this important?"

The ground can give way and the whole building will fall.

"Have you ever seen what happens to a house when something has gone wrong with the foundation?"

Share any stories they have about this last question.

You

"Just like the foundation of a home is important to a home's stability during stressful times so it is important for our lives to be built upon a good foundation."
"Turn to Matthew 7:24-29. Let's read this together.

Them

Have someone read the entire parable.

Discovery:

You

"Jesus uses a short parable to conclude His Sermon on the Mount. A parable is just an extended simile where something is being compared with something else. In this parable, Jesus uses the term "house" as a figure of speech for something else. What do you think it refers to?"

Them

A person's whole life.
(Keep the discussion going by asking what else Jesus might have in mind until someone says the answer.)

207

"Since we have found one figure of speech in this passage, do you see any others?"

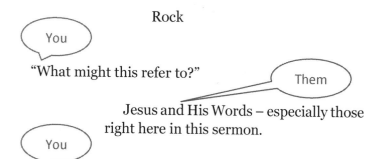

Scan down the next two pages for the different responses you are looking for and how to respond:

Rock

"What might this refer to?"

Jesus and His Words – especially those right here in this sermon.

"Let's take a minute to look at another passage that relates to this topic. Turn to I Corinthians 3:10-15. Would someone read this for us?" After reading it say, "Describe the foundation that Paul identifies here."

It is Jesus Christ. There is no other foundation for life. Also, others are building upon it and each of these builders will have his or her work tested in the end.

"Turn back to Matthew 7:24-27. Do you see any other figures of speech here and what do you think they might represent?"

Responses to look for:

Sand – the words of man like the
Pharisees.

Rain, Floods, Wind – the
challenges, difficulties, and
suffering we all experience in life.

"One of the key reasons for using a parable is to bring a person to a point of decision. It is designed to bring the hearer up short and cause them to respond to what was just said. In this case that involves the entire Sermon on the Mount. In Matthew chapter 7 Jesus gives two other illustrations. In each case Jesus makes a contrast.

First, let's look at Matthew 7:13-14, 'What is contrasted here?'"

Two different destinies for mankind.

"What are the consequences of going through each gate?"

One gate is wide and leads to
destruction. This is the gate most choose.
Another gate is narrow and leads to life
but few find it.

"Look at Matthew 7:15-23. Would someone read this?" (After reading it.) "What is contrasted here?" "And what is to be understood from this?"

You can know a person by the fruits of his or her life as to whether that person is a believer or not.

"In Matthew 7:21 Jesus states what may seem like a hard saying. What is it?"

Those who call Him Lord and do miraculous things think they are God's people but they aren't because they don't do His will and don't actually know Him.

"If you call someone 'Lord' would it be expected that you would treat that person accordingly and do what they say?"

Yes

Why?

If that person is the "Lord" he is the master. He is to be listened to and obeyed.

"What does it say here that Jesus expects from those who call Him Lord?"

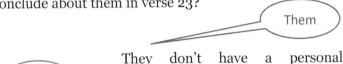

They would do what He says – obey Him – do His Word.

"Since they don't do what He expects what does Jesus conclude about them in verse 23?"

They don't have a personal relationship with God.

"The Sermon on the Mount begins in Matthew 5:1 with Jesus sitting down up on the mountain and His disciples coming to Him to listen to His words. When the writer notes that this happens on a 'mountain' that is a signal that what is about to be said is very important. The primary audience for this discourse was the disciples – those who were believers. No doubt others heard these words too because of the response of the people stated at the end of the sermon. The word used to describe the people's or crowd's response was 'amazed' and has the idea of one who is 'overwhelmed'. While the Pharisees would quote other authorities to make their points, Jesus simply stated the points making Himself the authority. This caught the crowd by surprise. So, considering what we started with in Matthew 7:24-27, what are we to learn about how to build our lives as believers from this passage?"

Believers who now are being transformed into His likeness, being readied for His Kingdom, acting wisely and not foolishly, and enduring life's challenges, difficulties, and suffering to His glory are ones who listen to and follow Jesus' words.

You

"Those who know God live like it now. They live according to God's words. In a very real sense, this entire sermon from Matthew 5-7 is all about what a true believer, disciple, looks like. It is about biblical transformation. At the heart of the sermon is the teaching on the devotional life as this is the key to all sustainable transformation for every believer. What is also interesting is that the whole book of Matthew is really a manual on discipleship. There are five discourses that Jesus gives in this book. And the very first discourse has prayer at its very center."

Decision

You

"It is with this in mind that I want to introduce you to the book, "*His Heart, My Heart – Devotional Transformation*" (Hand them out or make sure everyone has obtained one.)

"You should read the Introduction, Chapter 1 and 2 in the next few days. Starting tomorrow you are to begin doing one devotional a day for the next forty days. The first day's devotional starts after chapter two. Remember, God is the one who is drawing you to Himself! (cf. John 6:44; Philippians 2:13; Galatians 4:6). You are doing this out of delight and in humble response to His working within you. He wants you to develop your personal relationship with Him out of delight. It is important that you do not do this as something to check off a "to do list" – because you must do it. If you start this way you must come to the end of yourself (humble yourself before Him) before you will see the transformational impact of this practice upon your life.

Ideally, you should act out of love for God. But don't wait until you have the right motivation to begin. Ask God to properly motivate you as you begin and trust Him to show up. You will be amazed at how He will work the willingness and delightful desire to long to meet with Him into your life if you will let Him."

"Does everyone know what we are to do for next time?"

"Please bring this devotional with you to the next meeting!"

Close in group prayer. Ask everyone for things to pray for and either you collect them and pray for all of them or you ask people to remember the request from the person on their left and pray for that request in a few minutes. Mention who will open the prayer time and share that you will close it. This enables you to pray for any missed requests if needed.

His Heart, My Heart
Discussion #2

THE DEVOTIONAL LIFE AS A VITAL SIGN OF SPIRITUAL LIFE

Vision for Leaders:

One of the very first signs of spiritual life – the new birth – is a desire to communicate with God as one's Father (cf. Galatians 4:6). This cry, actually a loud shout, of "Abba! Father!" is God prompting the believer to pray. As a result, the devotional life is prompted by God. He moves a believer to prayer and places in them a hunger and thirst for God's Word (cf. Galatians 4:6; I Peter 2:2). Keep in mind in this session that you are encouraging believers to listen to and respond to God and what He is trying to do in each believer's life. In addition, this first week of devotions brought up whether a believer could approach God as his or her Father in light of their experience with his or her earthly father. You will want to explore this in this session.

Focus:

The devotional life is Spirit prompted, its importance can be caught but it must be taught to be biblically practiced. It draws a believer into communication with God as his or her Father.

Goals:

To know what the devotional life is from Matthew 6:5-13, that it is a vital sign of spiritual life from Galatians 4:6 and I Peter 2:2, and that every believer will experience the desire to talk with God as one's Father.

215

To feel delighted to be in God's family, to call Him Father and to spend time getting to know Him and becoming like Him through God's Word.

_To do_ - Call God Father without any hesitancy, begin resolving any false concepts about God as Father due to one's earthly father, and to be delighted to daily meet with God by continuing to do one daily devotional in the _"His Heart, My Heart 40-Day Devotional on Devotions"_ each day.

Approach: Prepare Your Group

(Leader's Note: The purpose of the Approach section is to get to know each person better, get their minds where their bodies are now, introduce the topic, and raise a real need to a felt need level.)

Tools needed for this session: You will need a small, hand size, soft ball to start this group. If you don't have one use a small pillow.

"Think for a moment about your earthy father. What is 'one word' that you would use to describe him? Don't say it now. This ball (small pillow) will determine who shares the word they picked for their father. When this is tossed to you share one word that best describes your relationship with your earthly father now. After you share your word toss this to someone else who hasn't shared. I'm going to start, since I have the ball."

Everyone shares one word that describes their earthly father.

You

"This time I want you to share one word that you wish was true of your relationship with your father. Again, I will start with the ball (or small pillow)."

Them

Everyone shares.

You

"Do you think that your experience with your earthly father has affected your view of God as your heavenly Father? How?

(Note: Don't toss the ball around this time, just give them some time to respond on their own. Allow some silence between responses and just ask if anyone else wants to share. Don't require everyone to speak. When the talking obviously dwindles tell the group that you are going to pray for them as they begin looking at the scripture for this session. Ask that God would speak to each heart during this session.)

Them

Give time for those who want to share to do so.

(Leader's note: If you are meeting with only one other person you can still ask the questions above but you should always share first and then ask the other person if they want to share.)

Discovery: A Group Discussion

"On a scale of 1 to 10 with 1 meaning 'I have to' and 10 meaning 'I want to' what number best represents your attitude towards spending time with God?"

Everyone shares a number.

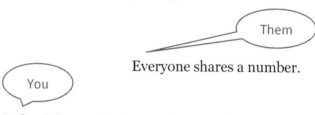

"Why did you pick the number you did?"

Have several share – you don't have to have everyone respond.

"What would it take to move it to a 10?"

Various responses.   Once there is silence for a bit, move on to the next question.

"How did you learn to spend time with God?"

(Use these Follow-up Questions as needed: Did anyone teach you? Have you seen it modeled? Was the teaching and/or modeling helpful to you? Why or why not?)

Various responses. Once there is silence for a bit, move on to the next question. Don't forget to listen carefully to each response as it will say a lot about that person and where they are in his or her walk with God!

"If you were to teach someone how to spend time with God, how would you do it?" "Would it make a difference whether the person was a new believer or an older one in the faith?"

Various responses. Listen carefully. Once there is silence for a bit, move on to the next question.

"Turn to Matthew 6:5-13. Let's read this together."

(Divide the verses up for everyone to read some. After reading this continue with the next question.)

"During the first seven days of this devotional you covered Matthew 6:5-9. It is here in Matthew 6:5-13 that Matthew records Jesus' teaching on how to pray. In Luke 11:1-4 the disciples ask Jesus to teach them how to pray like John taught his disciples. Prayer was a normal part of John the Baptist's ministry. And as Jesus' disciples watched Him pray they could see that it was important

219

but they didn't understand what to do. Therefore, they ask Him to teach them so that they could do it. As you look at Matthew 6:5-13, do you think spending time with God is optional, a good suggestion, highly advised, or expected?

Them

Expected – see use of "when" in the text at v5.

You

"From this passage, where should you meet with God?"

Them

Privately and in a place free of distactions – like a closet.

You

"From this text, when or how often should you meet with God?"

Them

Daily as found in v.11 and before eating.

You

"How do you feel about this point?"

Them

Various responses. Listen carefully for resistance, teachability, and submissiveness. Promote a humble response to God's word and Him having His way in our lives.

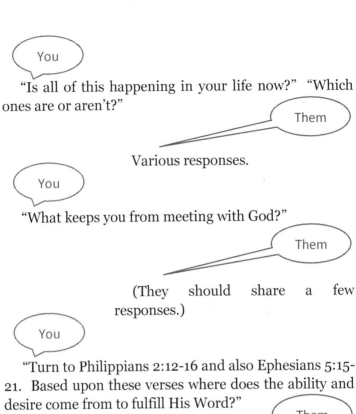

You

"Is all of this happening in your life now?" "Which ones are or aren't?"

Them

Various responses.

You

"What keeps you from meeting with God?"

Them

(They should share a few responses.)

You

"Turn to Philippians 2:12-16 and also Ephesians 5:15-21. Based upon these verses where does the ability and desire come from to fulfill His Word?"

Them

You

The Holy Spirit living in a believer/follower of Christ.

"What does it mean if we aren't making time to meet with God?"

Them

We aren't getting time in God's Word, we aren't listening to Him, we won't know what He is wanting to do in and through us.

You

"Are we still filled with the Spirit if we aren't making

time for God? Look at Galatians 4:6. What do you think?"

Nope

You

"According to Galatians 4:6, what is the Holy Spirit doing in us?"

Them

Drawing us to talk with God as our Father.

You

"In the first seven days of this devotional there were a number of passages mentioned where God was referred to as our Father. Do you think that knowing God is your Father is an important factor in moving you to pray?" "Why or why not?"

Them

Various responses but you should hear something to the effect that the Father is the one a believer longs to spend time with and get to know.

You

In Matthew 6:9 it says, "Pray then like this: Our Father, in heaven. Hallowed be Your name." "What does it mean to call God your Father?" "Before you respond, think about the verses mentioned at the beginning of the first seven days of this devotional to answer this question."

I'm part of a new family. I have access to the very throne room of God where my Father meets with me. I am welcomed as His child. My Father longs to hear from me as He draws me to Himself.

"How do you see Him when you meet with Him? Do you see Him as your Father? Why or why not?"

Various responses. (Leader's note: listen to these responses and see if you need to follow-up and talk privately about anything that was shared in response to this question and the next one.)

"What struggles do you have with calling God Father?"

Various responses.

Decision: Ending Your Small Group Time

"From spending time with God over the last seven days, what is one thing that was helpful or that you want to remember?"

(Leader's note: if they haven't been using the devotional encourage them to be faithful to do one devotional a day. Work towards helping them be accountable to this. Talk about the next question and suggest ways that each person could help each other daily make time with God a priority.)

Various responses

You

"What is one thing we could do as a group (or that I could do) that would help you be better at practicing the devotional life?"

Them

Various responses but if someone shares an area they want help with you need to ask them: What is it? What would you like me (us) to do? The goal here is to hold each other accountable to reach the goal that God has placed upon their heart.

(Leader note: End your time with prayer for each other.)

"One of the things we should include in our time with God is time praying for others. Let's take a few minutes and pray for each other. What are some things on your heart today?"

Them

Either you pray for all that is shared or

have them pray for the person's request
on their left after everyone has shared and
then you close the whole time.

His Heart, My Heart
Discussion #3

NEW DISCIPLE'S DEVOTIONAL LIFE

Vision for Leaders:

In this session, you will discuss the typical New Disciple's devotional life. This is done by focusing on the first and fourth petition in the Disciple's prayer: Hallowed be Your Name and give us this day our daily bread. You will look at how knowing who God is and trusting Him develops faith that one's basic needs will be met. A typical new believer is still getting to know God and that He can be trusted. During this time, it is not uncommon to find "little faith" as defined in our text – Matthew 6:25-34 – note especially verse 30. It is also important to see the connection between trust and our new family. Trust is best developed in the context of a family. If there is not a sense of being part of His family there will be little trust developed until there is assurance of one's faith.

Focus:

New disciples grow from little faith to faith in God as Father, honoring His name because of who He is and what He does, learning that He can be trusted with meeting one's life's basic needs.

Goals:

To know how to honor God's name, grow in one's faith, and trust God to meet one's basic needs for life.

To feel loved by Him, assured of being in His family, and show one's love for Him by praising His name.

To do life by always honoring His name, telling

227

Him who He is and what He has done in prayer and by trusting in Him by faith to provide one's basic physical needs by thanking Him for doing this.

Approach: Prepare Your Group

Take time to help your group members get their minds where their bodies are now. **Pick only one** of the options below to start your group.

Option #1 - Ask your members to think back over the last week of personal times with God. Describe how they went using amusement park terminology – i.e. it was like a Ferris Wheel some up and some down; it was like a merry-go-round it didn't go anywhere; it was like a roller coaster everyday was different and exciting; etc.

You

Option #2 – Think about your name. Do you know what it means? Ask students to share what their name means. Then ask them if knowing what their name means makes a difference in how they think about themselves or act.

After the activity above, begin your group time with prayer. Ask one person to pray for your time together. Again, mention that there will be time at the end to share requests and pray as a group.

Discovery: A Group Discussion

You

"Think for a minute about this question, 'How is God's name treated today?'"

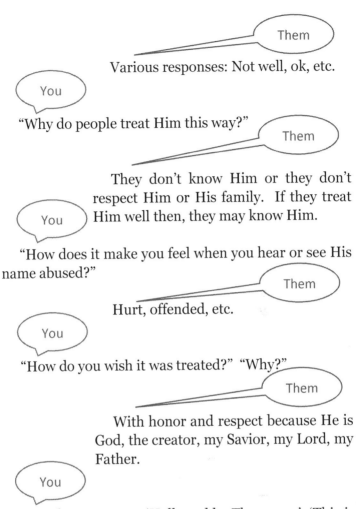

Them

Various responses: Not well, ok, etc.

You

"Why do people treat Him this way?"

Them

They don't know Him or they don't respect Him or His family. If they treat Him well then, they may know Him.

You

"How does it make you feel when you hear or see His name abused?"

Them

Hurt, offended, etc.

You

"How do you wish it was treated?" "Why?"

Them

With honor and respect because He is God, the creator, my Savior, my Lord, my Father.

You

"Matthew 6:9 says, 'Hallowed be Thy name.' 'This is the first request in our personal time with God.' 'Why start here with our time with God?' 'Why include this request at all?' 'What do you think?'"

Them

Need to start with the proper perspective.

"By putting this first what does it keep us from doing?"

Making this all about us. It should get our eyes off our situation and on to Him. And various other responses.

"Can you think of any reason that people wouldn't want God's name to be honored, treated as separate or holy?"

Them

Pride, sin, and other reasons.

You

"What role do you think 'self' wants to play in your time with God?"

Them

Self, under the control of the New Nature (God's indwelling in every believer) would want to yield to God. But if self is controlled by the flesh (the corruption from the sin nature still in us) then it will exalt itself over Him. It would want its way and not God's way. (This is a big area for discussing more from Romans 6-8 and will be addressed in a future discussion.)

"OK, time for some heart-searching questions: (Ask all the questions and then let them respond.)

'How do you treat His name?'

'Do you lift it up?'

'Do you want His name to be honored rather than your own?' 'How much more than your own?'

'Are these hard questions?' 'Why?' or 'Why not?'"

Various responses including: maybe I don't treat His name well or speak it in an acceptable manner, maybe I want my name to be recognized more than God's, flesh wants to exalt itself and wants the honor, and these are hard questions because they reveal how sinful I can be.

"It says in Matthew 6:9 that we are to direct these requests to our Father 'who is in heaven.'" "When you meet with God do you picture yourself coming into His presence in heaven – into His throne room?" "Why or why not?"

Them

Various responses including: I've always thought of Him coming to where I am rather than me going to where He is.

"Does it make a difference how you picture yourself meeting with God?"

It probably does. If He is coming to me then that makes Him close to me and seems to make me more of the focus, then Him. If I'm coming into His throne room in heaven where He is then that changes my focus from my earthly concerns to realizing who He is and the privilege it is as His child to come where He is at now.

"When you picture God being in heaven, what comes to mind?"

Various responses including: God on His throne in heaven surrounded by the heavenly host ready to do whatever He says to them.

You

"Now, realize that when you meet with God it is just you and Him." "How do you feel when you picture God this way?"

Them

Blessed and privileged.

You

"Do you think there is a relationship between how you see God and not worrying about your basic physical needs being met?" "What is it according to Matthew 6:25-34?"

Them

God can be trusted to take care of my physical needs. He is my Father and knows what I need before I ask Him. His character can be trusted.

You

"Do you find it hard or easy to trust God for your basic needs?" "Why or why not?"

Them

Various responses.

You

"What might a lack of being satisfied with how God meets your physical needs indicate about how you see God?"

Them

That I don't think that He knows what is best for me. That I'm not trusting Him. Other responses.

You

"What can you do to build a greater trust in God and be more content with what He does do?" "Someone look up Psalm 9:10, Hebrews 13:5 and Romans 10:17." (Have someone read each verse and then discuss how it helps you address this question.)

Them

We need to be content with what we have. God is with us. He is enough. He can be trusted to give us what we need. Our trust grows as we spend time in His Word.

Decision: Ending Your Small Group Time

"What have you learned this week about spending personal time with God?"

Them

Various responses

You

"What is one thing you believe God is telling you to focus on in your devotional life now?"

Them

Various responses – ask those who don't share anything what they are thinking. Get everyone to share at least one specific thing.

You

"When and how will you do it?"

Them

Various responses but you must ask them to be specific here. You may need to ask them for more specifics and for a time when they will do it.

You

End your time with prayer for each other after everyone has shared. You can close the group or have everyone pray for the person on their right and their request and then you close after everyone has prayed.

His Heart, My Heart
Discussion #4

GROWING DISCIPLE'S DEVOTIONAL LIFE

Vision for Leaders:

As a believer begins to trust God and grow from little faith to faith in God he or she will move from a self-focus to an others-focus. During this session, you will explore the relationship between the petitions: Your Kingdom Come and Forgive us our debts as we forgive those who trespass against us. A Growing Disciple is learning what life is like in God's Kingdom with Him reigning as King. As a result, they become interested in community relationships and how to maintain biblically healthy community. This requires the experience of vertical forgiveness with God and horizontal forgiveness with others. The areas of offense are discovered by exploring God's Kingdom rule, what He approves of and what He doesn't. This is all based upon His nature as God – the rules are based upon His character and nature not a random set of standards, not a majority vote, or man's creation. In God's Kingdom you rise up to align your life with Him and His way of living. Truth determines what your experience is to be when He reigns and your experience does not define truth like in our current culture. It is in this stage of discipleship that you see the most transformation in a believer's life. This is when they become change agents and servants within the body of Christ for His glory.

Focus:

Growing disciples live in alignment with God and His kingdom in forgiving, peaceful and loving community with others and for others rather than for self. They align their lives with God's truth and see their experience change – this is true biblical transformation.

Goals:

    <u>To know</u> that Jesus is King, discover the nature of His Kingdom rule and to know how believers are to live in forgiving and loving relationships with one another and think more highly of others than themselves.

    <u>To feel</u> humble before God as King knowing that he or she is a forgiven and significant child of the King in meaningful community with one another.

    <u>To do</u> what is necessary to keep the unity of the body of Christ in the bond of peace by following God each day, forgiving others and seeking other's forgiveness as needed which is all prompted by daily time with God, pursuing Him and His ways, with His resources, as each believer practices the devotional life every day.

Approach: Prepare Your Group

    Take time to help your group members get their minds where their bodies are now. **Pick only one** of the options below to start your group.

    Option #1 – Think about different kingdoms that have come and gone: The Persian Kingdom, The Roman, etc. How would you identify that a kingdom exists? What does it take to have a real kingdom? How different are kingdoms from one another? What makes them different?

Option #2 – Ask each person in your group to play a role of someone in a kingdom. Have these kingdom roles written on a piece of paper before your small group meeting: The King, A Son of the King, A Daughter of the King, A Servant, A Master/Lord, A Foreigner, A Repentant Prisoner, A Rebellious Prisoner. Do not tell the group the different roles. Hand out these roles and then go around the room and have each person tell their perspective of the kingdom based on their role but without revealing it. Each person should only have one role to play. Now have each person try to guess what role in the kingdom each person is playing. Be sure to remind each person not to reveal their role as they share their perspective of the kingdom. Ask people to be creative in playing their role.

Option #3 – Describe a time when you were caught doing something you weren't supposed to be doing. What happened? How did you feel? How did it turn out? Who was the authority figure in your story? Why did you feel accountable to that person? How did your actions affect your relationship with that individual? How is it today?

You

After doing one of the activities above begin your group time with prayer. Ask one person to pray for your time together. Again, mention that there will be time at the end to share requests and pray as a group.

Discovery: A Group Discussion

"When you think of a kingdom what comes to mind?"

A king, servants, the king's family, a castle, a throne, etc.

"What comes to mind when you think of God's Kingdom?"

Them

Jesus, God the Father, the church – the bride of Christ, the new heavens and earth, the city of God, etc.

You

"Let's think a bit deeper about this question." "What comes to mind when you think of God's Kingdom coming to earth?"

Them

Various responses.

You

"From what vantage point or perspective in your own mind do you tend to watch it happen or view its establishment as you think about it?" "Are you far away watching the whole thing take place?" "Are you next to Jesus as He begins to reign?" "Are you in a huge audience suspended in space with the King,

Jesus at the center?" "Where do you see yourself?" "What do you see?" "Try to describe it."

Them

You Give everyone a chance to say how they picture this.

"What are your feelings as you watch this happen?" "Why do you feel this way?"

Them

You Energized, fearful, scared, excited, etc.

"Turn to Hebrews 12. Look at verses 22 through 29." "What type of kingdom do you belong to based upon these verses?" "How would you describe it?"

Them

You An unshakeable kingdom. One where Jesus reigns and all the host of heaven are there along with us.

"What is your relationship to the King in this kingdom according to James 2:5, I Peter 2:9-10, Revelation 5:9-10, and 20:6?"

Them

An heir of the kingdom – James 2:5. A chosen race, royal priesthood, holy nation, the people of God, ones who have received mercy, a people for God's own possession so we can proclaim the excellencies of Him – I Peter 2:9-10. Priests who reign with God – Revelation 5:9-10; 20:6.

239

"Does this relationship we have to the King make any difference in how we live now on earth?" "Why or why not?"

It should. We should live now like the one we represent.

"According to 2 Peter 3:14, should it make a difference?" "How?" "Look at 2 Peter 3:14-18."

Them

Peter says that these believers "long for" or "are waiting for" the coming new world where righteousness reigns – that is God's kingdom in full force here on earth. Peter then says that since they have this longing they should live now like they want it by being at peace with God, spotless in character, blameless in conduct. We should also see His delay in bringing judgement as an opportunity for people to respond to the gospel and be saved (cf. 2 Peter 3:9 and 15). We should also beware of false teachers and guard ourselves from them and grow in our knowledge of God.

You

"If you were the King of a kingdom how would you handle those who disobeyed?"

Various responses

"How does our disobedience to God as our King affect Him?" "What does Paul say about this in Ephesians 4:30?"

Them

It grieves Him.

You

"What does Paul also note in I Thessalonians 5:19?"

Them

It stops His work in us.

You

"John says what God has done to address sin in our lives in I John 2:1-2." "What has He done?"

Them

He has provided for this by Christ's death. He is our defense attorney.

You

"According to Hebrews 12:4-11 how does God deal with disobedience of His children in the Kingdom?"

Them

He disciplines us.

"What should we do to keep from disobeying God according to Hebrews 12:12-13?"

We need to develop self-control and perseverance which is discipline in the areas which are weak.

"What do we need to do to restore family fellowship if we have disobeyed God according to I John 1:9, Psalm 32:1-5, Matthew 5:23-24, and Ephesians 4:32?"

We need to confess our sin to God – agree with Him that it is wrong and repent and choose to depend on Him. We need to ask for forgiveness from others when we have offended them. We need to forgive others who ask us to forgive them.

Decision: Ending Your Small Group Time

"In the next few moments I want you to take some time to allow God to speak to you." "In order to do this let's turn to Psalm 139 and read through the entire Psalm verse by verse." "Just read one verse and we will continue until we are done."

Them

Read the entire Psalm

You

"I'm going to read Psalm 139:23-24 again and this time make this your own prayer." "Let God search your heart. Whatever He brings to mind is exactly what He wants you to deal with in your life. It may have already come to your mind what He wants you to focus on at this time. As He reveals things don't argue or rationalize them away or ignore them. Instead realize that what has come to mind is exactly what God wants to deal with in your life right now. Confess or admit to God that these things are wrong. Ask Him to forgive you and cleanse you from all guilt." (Read Psalm 139:23-24 and give them time to privately let God point anything out to them. After a few moments read Psalm 103:12 and then say:

"Take a minute to personally thank God for paying the price for your forgiveness on the cross. Thank Him for forgiving you." (After a brief time say the next statement below.)

"Since God has forgiven you, what should you do for others according to Ephesians 4:32 and Matthew 6:14-15? (Forgive them)

Is it easy or hard to forgive other people? Why?

Why is it important that we forgive others?
"Can you think of someone you need to forgive?"

"When will you tell them that you forgive them?"

243

"Who will hold you accountable to do this?"

"Can we/I ask you next week if you did this?"

End your time with prayer for each other. Ask for prayer requests. Spend time praying for each other.

His Heart, My Heart
Discussion #5

MATURE DISCIPLE'S DEVOTIONAL LIFE

Vision for Leaders:

As a believer becomes mature in his or her faith they will seek to do God's will in His power, overcome all obstacles to accomplishing God's will – being victorious over the resistant flesh and the snares of the Devil – and will do so even if it might cost them their physical life – thus a real Christian martyr.

Focus:

Mature disciples seek to do God's will in the power of the Holy Spirit, overcoming the flesh and the devil's snares, even if it might cost them their own physical life.

Goals:

To know what God's will is and how to depend upon the power of the Holy Spirit to overcome the resistant flesh and the Devil's snares to do it.

To feel confident and stable in knowing God's will and sense God's supernatural power working God's will through him or her to God's glory.

To do what God wants in His power moment by moment, decision by decision, by walking in the power of the Holy Spirit by faith by daily spending time with God and praying at all times.

Approach: Prepare Your Group

Pick from one of the options below to start your group.

Option #1 – Write the name of a different tool on separate pieces of paper. You should have enough so each person in your group has three pieces of paper (three different names of tools). Go around the room and have each person select one of their tools and tell how that tool is useful, what training is needed to use it and what has to be done to keep the tool ready to use. After everyone has shared a tool then go back around and have everyone share the type of person who uses this tool the best in their occupation. Then ask, "Does it make a difference whose hand the tool is in for the best results?" "Why?" (Options for tool names: hammer, screw driver, electric saw, hand saw, gas powered lawn mower, hedge trimmer, garden hose, microwave oven, coffee maker, curling iron, electric razor, hand razor, iron, ironing board, butchers knife, race car, climbing rope, road bike, airplane, rocket, bullet proof vest, scuba tank, snorkel, swimming fins, arm floats, electric drill, scalpel, paint ball gun, make-up, tweezers, toothbrush, violin, piano, flute, guitar, drums, flashlight, spot light, laser beam, etc.)

Option #2 – Have each person in the group tell how they learned to drive a car. What was the hardest thing to remember to do? How long did it take to get it right? What would have happened if you had decided not to do that part of driving correctly? What is the most embarrassing thing you have done as a driver?

Option #3 – Create your own activity to start this lesson.

You

Next, begin your group time with prayer. Ask one person to pray for your time together. Mention that there will be time at the end to share requests and pray as a group.

Discovery: A Group Discussion

"In a sense, you are a tool in God's hand. What do you think and feel about being in God's hand and that He is using you for His purposes?"

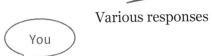

Privileged, loved, etc.

"Do you feel ready to be a vessel who can be used by God?" "Why or why not?"

Various responses

You

"Turn to Romans 12:1-2. Would someone read it for us?"

Them

(Have someone read this passage.)

You

"Based on this passage what is the first step in being a useful tool in God's hand?"

We present our bodies to God as a living sacrifice for Him.

"Once we have given our whole body to Him to use for His glory, what are we to do next to be ready to be used by God?"

Be transformed with the renewing of our mind so we can prove God's will is perfect.

"Think about this phrase, 'Knowing God's will and doing it.' Which part of it is easy to do? Which part is hardest to do? Why?"

Various answers.

"Turn to Ephesians 5:15-17. What does it say?"

(Have someone read the passage.)

"Before moving on we need to know what the meaning is of this phrase, 'understand what the will of God.' In this passage the word, 'understand' in the Greek means to know by perception, to join the

248

perception with the thing perceived. It connects what we understand with our minds to real life. We need to know or understand what He wants and then see how it relates to or applies to real life situations. The word for will means that which is willed – objectively. Where do we find God's will?"

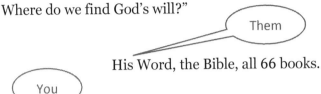

His Word, the Bible, all 66 books.

"It is in God's Word we find His will. As a result, we need to be good at biblical interpretation. This will involve observing the text, interpreting it, and then applying it correctly to a real-life opportunity."

"What could we do to establish a habit of getting into God's word so we will continue to grow in knowledge of His will on a regular basis?"

Learn how to study God's Word, interpret it, and apply it. Have a weekly plan to study it. Have someone keep me accountable to do it.

"Let's compare two passages: Ephesians 5:17-21 and Colossians 3:16-17. Would someone read the Ephesians passage and someone else the Colossians text?"

Read both passages

"What is the relationship between "word-filling" in the Colossians passage and "Spirit-filling" in the Ephesians passage?"

Them

They both result in the same effects: singing, sharing with others, thankfulness and submission.

You

"Why do you think they both result in the same effects?" "What does this say about the relationship between them?"

Them

They must be connected in some way.

You

"If God's word was the 'gas' for your car and the Holy Spirit was the 'engine' how would you describe the importance of each and how they worked together?"

Them

The engine depends on the gas to run but the engine does all the work. You can only be filled with the Spirit as much as you are filled with God's Word.

"Is there a difference between having an engine in your car and depending upon the engine to move your car?"

Sure, the engine doesn't do any good unless you use it.

"In the same way, is there a difference between having the Spirit of God resident in your life versus Him being president of your life? What is the difference?"

Yes, in one case He is in charge and in the other case He is just present. Being present is important because it means you are a believer – the Spirit lives in you. But when He is leading you moment by moment and decision by decision then He is being president of your life too.

"Here are some things we have been talking about. First, the difference between being indwelt by the Spirit and being filled with the Spirit. Notice in the Ephesians 5:17-21 passage that it describes some general results of being filled with the Spirit. They are speaking to one another in psalms and hymns, making melody in your heart to the Lord, being thankful in all things and being subject to one another. This is found in Ephesians 5:19-21. But there is also a specific result of being filled with the Spirit based upon Ephesians 5:17 which I leaped over. Think about the last time you confessed something to God that you failed to do or did wrong. Why would you confess it and ask God to fill you with His Spirit? It is because you can't do His will in your power and you want to re-establish your relationship with God and now live in His power. This means that knowing God's will from His Word is critical to being filled with the Spirit. God wants to empower you to do it. Therefore, when you are filled with His power what should that enable you to do?"

It means I am now able to do His will which is His Word or I will now be able to do what I just confessed I failed to do or did wrong.

You

"Turn to Galatians 2:20. Would someone read that verse for us?"

Them

Read the verse

You

"Based on this verse, how are we to live our lives?"

Them

By faith.

You

"Faith is confidence or trust in a reliable object. It is based upon evidence that can be trusted. God's Word can be trusted and we can trust Him to empower us to do what He says. So, the specific result of being filled with the Spirit is that we know God's will, understand it, and see how it relates to real life and then in His Power find the supernatural strength to do it by faith. We should be able to turn around after confessing a sin and do by faith in His strength what we just failed to do or did wrong! This is how transformation begins to get traction in our daily lives. It also means we need to be alert and disciplined in responding to Him working in us."

Decision: Ending Your Small Group Time

Make copies or write out this next paragraph for each group member before class: (Have them read it and then ask the questions.)

It takes a step of faith for us to move from knowing God's will to doing it. This step of dependence upon Him takes some risk. We are trusting that God will show up and do in His power what we can't do in our own strength. But it also takes discipline – the exercising of self-control in what we are trusting God to do and then repeating it over and over which is perseverance so that we develop a godly Christ-like habit.

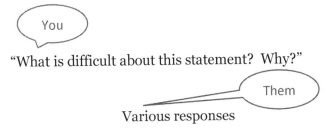

"What is difficult about this statement? Why?"

Various responses

You

"Can you think of a time in your life when you stepped out in faith and depended upon God to do something only He could do? Would anyone like to share their story?"

Them

(Give a few the opportunity to respond – be prepared to share one personal story to get things started if no one volunteers.)

You

"What are the biggest obstacles to doing God's will?"

Them

Fear, time, the world, flesh, and the devil.

You

"Which is the biggest obstacle for you?"

Them

Various responses

You

"Let's look up and read about how to deal with each challenge. Would someone read I John 4:18 about fear; Ephesians 5:16 about time; I John 2:15-17 about the world; Galatians 5:16 and Philippians 4:8 about dealing with the flesh; and I Peter 5:8-9 and James 4:7 about dealing with the Devil."

You

"How are we to deal with each one?"

Fear – if you love God we will not fear.

Time – we all have the same amount of time but we don't all have the same opportunities. So, we need to remember we are purchasing back from bondage to the Devil opportunities so God's will is done instead.

World – don't love it, it is temporary and passing away.

Flesh – walk in the power of the Spirit and control our thoughts by focusing upon what is true, right and lovely.

Devil – Resist him and he will flee.

"Which obstacle to doing God's will causes you the most problems?"

        Make sure everyone identifies one.

"What passage of scripture can you memorize to begin the process of having victory in this area?"

Help everyone find one passage from God's Word they can memorize this week that relates to their biggest challenge to obedience to God.

255

"Let's end our time with prayer for each other."
Spend time praying for each other and the area of
need they have expressed.

His Heart, My Heart
Discussion #6

GOD'S WORD AND PRAYER

Vision for Leaders:

Daniel 9 is an excellent place to show how all the aspects of the devotional life come together. In this session, you will see how Daniel got into God's Word and prayed. Note his passion for God and His ways. Note how he pursues God and intercedes for others. This session is meant to deepen the relationship between God's Word and the work of the Holy Spirit in prayer.

Focus:

God's word is the sword of the Spirit and prayer is driven and sustained by knowing His Word.

Goals:

To know how Daniel integrated God's Word into His devotional life of prayer and was lead into intercessory prayer.

To feel the necessity of using God's word in his or her devotional life of prayer.

To do the devotional life using God's Word as the foundation for it each day by systematically moving through it.

Approach:

Get a hand size, soft ball to bring to group.

"Over the last several weeks you have been walking though the book, **"His Heart, My Heart – Devotional Transformation."** As we toss this ball around I want you to share one thing God has talked to you about because of doing this study. I will start." (**Note to Leader**: Share what God said to you and what you are doing with what He has told you. Then toss the ball to someone else and ask them to respond to the question. Then that person tosses the ball to another person and it continues until everyone has had a turn. Only use the ball if you have more than five or more in your group.)

Discovery:

"Turn to Daniel 9:1-27. Let's go around the group and each one read a verse until we finish the passage."

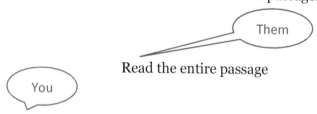

Read the entire passage

"Pair up with someone and look back over this passage. I want you to find all the elements of a healthy devotional life from this passage. Write down what you see and then we will collect your responses in a minute." (**Leader Note**: If your group is small or you are doing this one-on-one you should do this together and share what you find as you go. Just keep asking, "What else do you see here?")

Leader Note: Keep the list going until you have heard these:

Them

Spend time in God's Word
Pray
Honor God's name by telling Him who He is
  and what He does or has done.
Confess personal sin.
Confess sin of others.
Intercessory prayer for others.
Ask for God's forgiveness.
Ask God to do His word – His will.
Ask for God's help.

You

"Daniel's prayer should motivate us to read God's word and pray."

Decision: Use the ball again.

You

"Which elements are you finding it easy to do and which ones are you finding it hard to do or you aren't there yet?" (**Leader Note**: toss the ball around if your group is more than four.)

Them

Various responses

You

"How are you using God's Word – the Bible – in your devotional life?"

Various responses

"One of the best ways to use God's Word is to daily move through the entire Bible on a regular basis in your devotional life. There are several ways to do this. You could go through the whole Bible one verse at a time, one paragraph at a time, one chapter at a time. You could read a chapter from the Old Testament each day and a chapter from the New Testament each day. You could read a chapter in Proverbs each day and read a Psalm every day. The point here is to read the book in its context and in sequence so you work your way through the entire Bible over time and then repeat it. So, 'How will you use God's Word in your time with God tomorrow?' 'What will you do?' 'What will be your plan as you start getting into God's Word?'"

(**Leader Note**: Make sure everyone shares what they will do specifically. If it isn't specific you can't measure if it was done or not. Make sure what they are thinking of doing is achievable and not too much. Let them know that you will keep them accountable to their goals and ask them about it.)

"Last week we talked about memorizing a passage.

How have you been doing with that?"

(**Leader Note**: Find out how everyone has been doing with this and address any issues that arise. Ask them to continue this practice with another area of need or to finish memorizing the passage from last week.)

"What would you like prayer for today?"

(**Leader Note**: Pray for each other in the areas mentioned. Make sure you include what was shared about how they will get into God's Word starting tomorrow and what they said about how their memorizing the passage from last week was going.)

His Heart, My Heart
Discussion #7

DISCIPLESHIP COMMUNITY

Vision for Leaders:

As you lead this discussion you need to keep in mind that humans were made in the image of God (Genesis 1:27) and that one aspect of God's image is community. Men and Women were never meant for life alone but in relationship with others in order to reflect the ideal community: the Father, the Son and the Holy Spirit. Therefore, the ideal for human community is found in God and in the "one-another" statements in the Bible. Second, God designed us to grow together to maturity in community with others. This session sets the stage for on-going time together as a group committed to grow together into disciples who make disciples who make disciples.

Focus:

You were designed to need one another in biblical community to fully reflect being made in God's Image and to mature and multiply as disciples together.

Goals:

To know that you need one another, were meant to experience community like the ideal community of the Father, Son, and Holy Spirit, and make disciples.

To feel your need for biblical relationships with others in community.

To do daily devotions on your own, take the Stages of Discipleship Self-Evaluation, and continue meeting as a small group now focused on being moment by moment spirit-filled image bearers of God in biblical community who make disciples.

Approach:

Read the statement by George Gallup and ask the questions one at a time and give your small group members time to think and respond to each one.

You

George Gallup has said, "Americans are among the loneliest people in the world."
—George Gallup Jr., *The People's Religion* (New York: MacMillan, 1989).
"Do you agree or disagree? Why?"

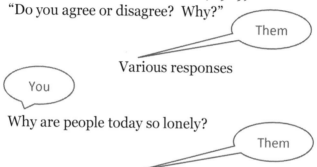
Them

Various responses

You

Why are people today so lonely?

Them

They think they have friends because they have hundreds of Facebook friends. They are lonely because they aren't spending face to face time with others. They lack communication skills to build relationships. Other responses....

You

"Do you think your friends and peers experience loneliness? Why or why not?"

Them

Various responses

"When was the last time you had a meaningful interaction with another person: family member, friend, neighbor, or stranger?"

Share as many stories as you have time for.

Discovery:

"Genesis 1:27 says people are made in God's image. (Read it to them.) God is three in one. To fully reflect His image, requires relationships with others. What would an ideal community look like?" "Describe it as best you can."

People would be open and honest.
They would move towards greater transparency.
They would speak truth to one another.
They would grow together.
They would care for each other, protect one another, and guide each other towards greater Christ-likeness.
Other responses...

"Turn to John 17. We will go around the group and read one verse at a time until we finish the chapter. As we do this think about what the ideal community looks like between Jesus, the Father, and the Holy Spirit."

(Read the passage.)

"What does an authentic meaningful community relationship look like?" "Identify as much as you can from Jesus' prayer to His Father that is true of the ideal authentically loving and meaningful relationship within the Godhead between the Father, Son and Holy Spirit." Using this passage how would you describe the ideal community?"

They all love one another.
Everyone does the role they are responsible to do with total satisfaction.
They support each other.
They praise each other.
They work together.
They bring others into the community.
Additional responses...

You

"Would someone find Hebrews 10:23-25? Someone else Philippians 2:1-4? And someone else Acts 2:43-47? As each passage is read think about what this text adds to what an authentic community relationship looks like."

Them

Pause after each passage is read and discuss what it adds to your understanding of true community.

Hebrews 10:23-25 – it is a community that holds to the same hope, they trust God to do what He promised, they seek to promote greater love and good works among every individual in the group, they meet together, they encourage each other.

Philippians 2:1-4 – they are encouraged in Christ, comforted in love, experience the Spirit together, there is affection and sympathy among them. They should be of one mind, one love, agree together, unselfish, not proud, humble, valuing others above oneself, and concerned about the interests of others.

Acts 2:43-47 – sharing with each other, time together in worship, eating together, joy, and growing in numbers.

"Biblical community is reflected in spirit-filled relationships with one another. There are several "one another" verses in the Bible. Each one describes a bit more about authentic community and how are we to interact biblically with one another. We are called in I Thessalonians 5:11 we are to encourage and build up one another. And because we are 'members of one another' in Ephesians 5:25 we are to 'speak truth' and do it in love so we grow together in verse 15. This community begins to look more and more like discipleship."

Decision:

(Note: A study of the 'one another' passages would be a good study to do on our own and then come back and discuss our findings. You could assign this here for another meeting where you launch your group into an on-going discipleship group. If you do this make sure you discuss the key truths or principles that are found next time.)

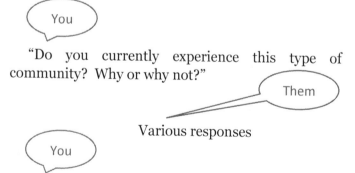

"Do you currently experience this type of community? Why or why not?"

Various responses

"Do you want this type of community with others? Why or why not?"

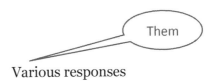

Various responses

"What could you do to promote better community with others?"

Various responses, then ask the next set of questions and get every person to specifically answer them. Note: if the answers to 'what they will do' question above isn't specific enough to be measurable or achievable you will need to get them to be more specific.

You

"When will you do this?"

"Who will hold you accountable to see if you did it?

After everyone has shared you should pray for each other's application and close the time.

269

Bonus Small Group Meeting
(This could be a meeting to launch into an on-going discipleship group.)

Vision for Leaders:
Take time to celebrate finishing this study. Have a special time together. Take time to share all God is doing in you and through you. Challenge them to continue on in being discipled.

Session Design:
As a leader, you need to note that these sessions have all involved the A.D.D. value to conversations lesson plan strategy. Here is your opportunity to create your own Approach (the A part of A.D.D.), Discovery (the first D in A.D.D.), and finally the Decision (the last D in this acrostic). As you develop your own lesson here are some things to include:
Encourage each disciple to walk through this book with at least one other person. First, ask them to do to help that person develop an eternal relationship with God and pursue Him and what is on His heart. Second, ask them to do it help make the truths of this practice more settled in their own lives as a leader of others. Finally, ask them to write out their plans in a letter to themselves. You should collect the letters and mail them back to each person at the end of the next 40 days. Remind them that by now they could have started to do this in someone else's life or with a small group and be almost to the point of encouraging their group or person to reproduce this practice with yet another group or individual.
Let's encourage others to purchase back out of bondage the opportunity for believers to daily meet with God and be prepared for opportunities

throughout the day that arise to redeem them for God rather than miss them and waste daily opportunities to pursue Him and His purposes.

Think of Moses' statement in Psalm 90:12, "So teach us to number our days, that we may present to You a heart of wisdom." Why are we to do this? Because our days are short. You can also remind them here of Ephesians 5:15, "Therefore, be careful how you walk, not as unwise men but as wise."

It all ties together. Let His Heart become what is passionately Our Heart. So, you can say with me every day, every moment, and every decision, "His Heart, My Heart."

Finally, take time to discuss Matthew 28:16-20. Make sure you listen to the session on the Great Commission at www.hisheartmyheart.org as you develop this lesson and challenge your members or individual to continue and be discipled by you while you lead another group through the **His Heart, My Heart – Devotional Transformation** book you just finished.

Appendix III

How to Understand God's Word and Transformational Bible Reading

Nothing is more important to a true disciple then hearing clearly from God. When we read the Bible, we need to realize that once an author has made a point, statement, or expressed what he wants to talk about there is only four things he can do after this. He can prove his point addressing the question "why?" He can explain his point addressing the question "what?" He can apply the point addressing the question "how?" He can also repeat the point using other words but only the first three methods will advance the author's argument. In light of this it should be your purpose to discover what the author is talking about first then discover how he develops his thoughts – the argument of the text – whether you are reading a psalm, narrative, epistle, gospel, or any other genre from the Bible or any other literary work.

Discover the Author's Big Idea

The discovery of what the author is talking about is what is called the subject of the Author's Big Idea. How he develops it is called the complement of the Author's Big Idea. To write the Author's Big Idea you need to study the text. Begin by reading the entire book in one sitting. Try this several times before you make a preliminary identification of what the author is talking about. You will want to take into consideration the structure of the book – its literary genre. There are different rules for how to interpret each structure but all of them will have a subject the author is addressing and something he is saying about it.

Let's just take the literary genre of Poetry. Poetry has

a unique structure. One of the characteristics of Hebrew Poetry – even Poetry in the New Testament shows this Semitic or Hebraic influence – is parallelism. For instance, Psalm 117 is talking about praising the Lord. But He is more specific than that. Notice in this short two verse psalm that all people are to do this. There are two lines here that are in parallel. One says, "all nations" are to praise the Lord and the next line says "all peoples" are to praise the Lord. Therefore, the complete subject is "Everyone should praise the Lord." Notice the two phrases "all nations" and "all peoples" can be expressed as "everyone". There are certainly implications to consider in light of this like, "What do the Gentiles have to praise the Lord about?" This question relates to the second part of the Author's Big Idea.

Once you discover what is being talked about it should be immediately or somewhat easily discovered what the author is saying about it. So, as you look at Psalm 117 what is the author saying about what he is talking about here? Do you think the author is explaining what it means to do this – answering the question "what?" Or is he applying this point by saying "how?" it is to be done? Or is he proving the point by saying "why?" it is to be done? Your answer to this will determine what is the complement to the Author's Big Idea. This is what the author is saying about what He is talking about. In this case the author is proving his point. He is talking about "why?" everyone should praise the Lord. It is because of His loyal unfailing love. You could have seen two reasons that the author gives here as to why everyone should praise the Lord but it is also likely here that just as in the first verse there was a parallel expression being used to call everyone to praise the Lord so here in the second verse it is possible that the two characteristics of God that are noted actually refer to His loyal, truthful, lasting love thus a parallel expression.

If this is a new idea to you that in poetry there are parallel expressions where meaning is repeated in some way then it would be a good time to read a book on how to understand the Bible. My purpose here however is to just point out how the Author's Big Idea – the actual meaning of the passage – is discovered and written in one sentence. So, in Psalm 117 the Author's Big Idea is, "Everyone should praise the Lord because of His loyal love and faithfulness."

So now that you know the question that the author addresses and the subject and how he develops it you can state it in one sentence. You can do this for a single verse, a paragraph, a chapter, and the entire book. You can do this for any literary genre not just Epistle. It is a bit for difficult to do this with Narrative but it is possible if you follow the rules of interpretation for that type of literature. I would suggest you get a book that addresses this or see my book, *Transformed by Truth* where I discuss the differences and help you through the book of Jonah.

For now, I suggest you try this with at least a paragraph when you are reading and studying an epistle or poetry. I suggest you read the entire scene that is in narrative to form the Author's Big Idea and realize that God is always the hero in narrative. Once you discover what the author was saying to the original audience you are now ready to apply it to your own life here and now.

Big Idea Today

In a day when there is a rush to personalize the text it is important to slow down and see what the author was really talking about and saying about it before we make that jump to what it means here and now to us. In light of Psalm 117's Big Idea how would you apply this to your life today? Would it help you to know that the concept of "praise" is always verbal and public when used in Hebrew, the language of most of the Old Testament? When was the last time you spoke well of God and His character verbally and publicly? When was the last time you told others the good news of God's loyal, faithful, and truthful love?

In this case the Author's Big Idea is the same as the Big Idea Today. What is the difference? The Author's Big Idea is what the text meant to the original audience in their culture, history, and geographical setting. When we take the Author's Big Idea and move the point into our culture, history, and geographical setting we need to think a bit more about whether or not what was said "then and there" is meant for us "here and now". What do I mean? Take the passage in Jeremiah 29:11, "'For I know the plans that I have for you,' declares the Lord, 'plans for welfare and not for calamity to give you a future and a hope." Does this apply directly to you "here and now?" Who was this written to? We must think about the original readers and the Author's Big Idea "there and then" before we can begin to think about us "here and now".

Now, you should know that Romans 8:28 assures us that God is working all things together for good for those who love Him so He does have a plan for you that is best for you. But note here that Romans 8:28 doesn't say everything we experience will be good only that what does happen to us will be used by God for good in our lives. He is a master at using even bad things to work good things into our lives. Now He also uses good things in our lives to work good things in our lives too. But you need to be comforted by the fact that God will meet you in your hour of need and use it for good in you (cf. Psalm 23 and 2 Corinthians 1:1-7). However, what do we do with Jeremiah 29:11?

The beginning of Jeremiah 29 identifies the cultural,

historical and geographical setting for these words as well as Jeremiah 29:10. Notice that the historical setting is the nation of Israel, God's people, are in captivity in Babylon. Notice that it is expected that this captivity will last for seventy years. According to Jeremiah 29:10 it will be at the end of the seventy years that God will visit His people and bring them back to Israel. It is in this context that Jeremiah has a word for God's people, v.11, "'For I know the plans that I have for you,' declares the Lord, 'plans for welfare and not for calamity to give you a future and a hope." This is great news to God's people. In fact, Daniel read this in his devotions in Daniel 9 as he realized that the seventy years were almost up. So, he prayed for God to do what His word said here!

Consider the Degree of Transfer

How do we today apply this text or do we? To address this issue, we need to consider the degree of transfer of this text to us "here and now." There are four possible options here: Universal; Similar; General; None.

If Jeremiah 29:11 is directly meant for us today, "here and now", then it would be a universal principle for all believers for all time. Should Peter have memorized this verse and applied it to himself when Jesus told him he would deny Jesus three times? Should martyrs of the faith through the ages or even in Revelation 6:11 use this verse in Jeremiah 29:11 as hope through persecution? Obviously, God had a different plan for Peter and for the saints in the book of Revelation since God is sovereign over all things (cf. Ephesians 1:11). The fact that God sovereignly controlled the length of time that Israel would be in captivity and that God would bring them back to their land was meant for them and not for us "here and now" so it isn't a universal principle for us today. We aren't in Babylon and haven't been out of the

Promised Land for seventy years and aren't promised the land either.

Could it be a similar principle for us today? If it is then we would have to be in some type of captivity like them (Babylon) and promised a return to a land we have been removed from (Israel). This is hard to see too. We need to not spiritualize the text to make it fit us today but actually see a real similar relationship.

Is this a general principle that works for us today? In this text, Jeremiah 29:11, God is concerned for His people and provides for them. We could say generally this is true for believers today. If we can't see a general principle, then there is no principle for us to apply today.

Now you should notice that there are so many texts that are directly applicable to believers today. In fact, the Great Commission says that the first disciples of Jesus were to teach others everything they heard from Jesus! This means that those who they taught were to do the same thing and it was to continue on through the centuries to us today.

So here is the point for reading the text well and interpreting it well. Discover what the author is talking about (the subject of the Author's Big Idea). Then find what the author is saying about what he is talking about (the complement of the Author's Big Idea). State these two things together in one complete sentence – this will be the Author's Big Idea of the text. It is the interpretation of the text "there and then."

Then ask questions about the Author's Big Idea as to whether the point is universal, similar, general, or not related at all to us today, "here and now."

If there is a relationship to us today, then you should be able to write the Big Idea Today in one complete sentence. Once you do this you are ready to apply this text to yourself today.

A Word About Applications

Realize that an application must be achievable, inspiring, measurable and shared to see real life transformation. First, achievable: this needs to be specific and something that can be done in the time limit identified in the measurable aspect of the A.I.M.S criteria. Second, inspiring: you should want to do this. Third, measurable: you must have a reasonable time limit identified with it. Finally, shared: someone else knows what your application is and is holding you accountable to do it. That means that person knows what to ask because your application is specific and measurable.

You are now on your way to see God do great things in and through you. Whatever you do stay in His Word and Pray. Walk daily with God. Enjoy the journey! Enjoy your eternal relationship with our incredible indescribable God.

HIS HEART, MY HEART TRANSFORMATIONS

Stay Connected!

Check out www.hisheartmyheart.org on the web and discover tools and training to help you make disciples who make disciples.

After completing this book, you should consider starting your own *His Heart, My Heart Cohort* using this book. As you lead the group discussions each week you will be helping others learn to do the devotional life and lay the foundation for real Christ-like transformation in each believer. One way to get a new group or several new groups started would be to schedule a **Devotional Transformation Seminar.** Check out the website above for details on this.

You should also be involved with a shepherd leader who can walk you through all the stages of discipleship. These type of leaders can identify where you are and lead you on to making disciples who make disciples. If you were in a small group to do this book, then ask the leader if they would be willing to help you identify someone who can do this with you.

Finally, become a shepherd leader who can take a believer through all the stages of discipleship so they make disciples who make disciples. See the **Shepherd Leadership Transformational Training Seminar** on the above website for details on this.

You can also stay connected by finding **His Heart, My Heart Transformations** on Twitter and Facebook.

Made in the USA
Columbia, SC
27 October 2017